TRAVELS
WITH
DAVID

ALSO BY DAVID FRENCH

Everything is Bad for You

Working Communally:
Patterns and Possibilities
(with Elena French)

for Meg and Jim,
fellow voyagers,
with love,
David

TRAVELS
WITH
DAVID

DAVID FRENCH

VAJRA PUBLISHING
SHELBURNE, VERMONT

ISBN: 978-0-692-75575-4
Cover and book design by Lindsay Francescutti

Printed in the United States of America

For Tana and Alex
and all the ways they have brought
life into the world.

CONTENTS

INTRODUCTION

At the end of 1960, I was a junior at Stanford University in northern California. Until then, my only travel outside the United States had consisted of a day as a tourist in Tijuana and Ensenada, Mexico. That wasn't unusual for the times. This was long before people began to travel internationally as easily as they traveled across town, and there were no "gap years" for students to bicycle or hitchhike across continents. The first U.S. Peace Corps volunteers would soon begin to find circuitous routes back home from their assignments overseas, and universities like Stanford were establishing campuses in Europe where students could spend a semester absorbing a new culture. But most young people stayed pretty close to home.

Things were about to change for me, though. My parents and brother were in Addis Ababa, Ethiopia, where my father was serving as the World Bank's Resident Representative. The Bank paid my way to visit them; and since Addis Ababa is on the other side of the planet from Palo Alto, I booked a trip around the world, with Addis as a lengthy stop mid-journey.

It was the beginning of a lifetime of travel. I've lived in 10 countries (on five continents) and done short-term work or traveled in 49 others. It has led me to interesting places, and I've described a number of these below. This doesn't amount to an autobiography – largely missing are accounts of my childhood, studies, relationships, marriage, writing, children – but rather involves a potpourri of travelogue, accounts of current events, descriptions of my professional life, and reflections on my state of mind and being along the way. I've pasted this together primarily with the thought that my grandchildren might someday like to see what Granddad had been up to, and that friends might be amused at some of my stories.

I've largely been limited to periods when I kept a journal, which means that big chunks of experience are neglected. I rather regret this. One way or another, though, most of what more than a half-century of traveling meant to me is reflected in what follows. There's no particular reason to read this in sequence, and there's more talk about work than you might find interesting. Skip around and see what you find.

Chapter 1

AROUND
THE WORLD

1960-1961

In late December 1960, I boarded a Pan American Airways flight in San Francisco that stopped in Honolulu and (as I remember) Wake Island before arriving at my first destination, Tokyo. I had more energy in those days: fresh off the overnight, 18-hour flight, I dealt with not being met as expected by a Japanese friend, somehow improvised a place to stay, and set off on a tour of the city. The whole five-month trip continued at much that tempo.

I was the compleat tourist: Kabuki drama in Tokyo, a charging rhino in Tanganyika (as it was then; it has since incorporated Zanzibar and become Tanzania), the Little Mermaid in Copenhagen Harbor, the lush Cambodian jungle near Angkor Wat, the Taj Mahal, the Addis Ababa mercato, Javanese opera in Djakarta, a walled village in Hong Kong, what I experienced as the "solid beauty" of the Parthenon. I registered predictable shock at the poverty and disease and blindness and disfigurement in some of these places, the people shitting at the side of the road, all the stuff you don't see much of in coastal America. Not a lot of special insight, just your all-American boy getting his feet wet for the first time.

What is a bit jarring is to imagine what has happened to some of those spots since I was there. The Angkor complex was a serene place with nobody much around; Bangkok was peaceful and uncrowded;

Addis was a patchwork of villages with nothing much going on; we had Tanzania's Ngorongoro Crater, a 100-square-mile game reserve, all to ourselves as we saw (according to my journal of the time) "8 rhinos, 24 lions, hundreds and thousands of gazelle, wildebeest, and zebra, hippos, 30-34 hyenas..." All those places are jammed with people and traffic now.

I seem to have been well connected, dining at the Royal Hong Kong Yacht Club and spending New Year's Eve at a ball at the Royal Bangkok Sports Club. Mostly, though, I took advantage of contacts to find things out from interesting people. In Hong Kong, for example, I had an introduction to someone at the American consulate, where I met with various officials during my time in town. In Bangkok, I stayed with the senior man at the Mekong River development project and attended a meeting he had arranged with the Minister for Foreign Affairs, representatives of all sorts of government agencies, a visiting mission from the Ford Foundation, and someone from the local World Bank office. In New Delhi, I lunched with the World Bank's Resident Representative and spent time (at his office and home) with the editor of the Eastern Economist.

Things continued in much that vein once I got to Africa. In Addis Ababa, I met a wide variety of local notables through my parents and was press liaison officer during an international conference. In Dar-es-Salaam, I had interviews with the Minister for Commerce and Industry, the Deputy Director of Education, and the American Consul-General. In Nairobi, I spoke with the USIS Cultural Affairs Officer, a Harvard dean, and somebody at the Kenya Broadcasting System. On the way back to Addis, Tom Mboya (a leader of Kenya's struggle for independence from the United Kingdom) spent much of the flight on the arm of the seat behind me, talking with friends while I eavesdropped.

I had no way of knowing how much all this would change my life. From my seat in the press balcony at the conference in Addis Ababa, I could see a young woman helping out in one of the African delegations. We had coffee together during breaks, and – one thing leading to many others – Elena and I were married in Massachusetts six years later. Among other eventual outcomes of those coffee breaks were our children (Tana and Alex) and grandchildren.

The several months of mini-immersion in Africa were also the beginning of a decades-long love affair with the continent. It determined the courses I took and later taught, the work I did over a lifetime, the places I lived, the people I met. Everything in the pages below is the outcome of those first months of my global travels.

TRAVELS WITH DAVID

Chapter 2
ABU SIMBEL, EGYPT
1963

Following my graduation from Stanford University in 1963, I took a summer internship with the U.S. Agency for International Development (AID) in Washington, D.C. I was planning to go on to Harvard University that fall to do graduate work in economics. I was unenthusiastic about the idea, but it would have given me an exemption from military service at a time when men were being drafted to be sent off to war in Vietnam, something I would never have accepted. (The alternatives would have been moving to Canada or going to jail.) Then two things happened: thanks to childhood polio and surgery later on the affected foot, I flunked my physical exam for the army; and AID offered me a job in Ethiopia. I had been captivated by Ethiopia during my family visit in 1961, and I jumped at the chance to take on a two-year assignment there. In October 1963, I arrived in Addis Ababa. Before really settling in, though, I had a side-trip to make.

The Egyptian riverboat had taken overnight to make it down the Nile from the Sudan border to Abu Simbel, the great temple devoted to the pharaoh Ramses II. It was informal travel, to say the least, with villagers and their animals getting on and off at apparently random points along the way. I slept on deck after hanging out with a disreputable group of expatriates who were coming from God knows where and heading for the same. Finally, we pulled up to the shore in the shadow of four towering statues of Ramses. I got off (the only person to do so), the boat left, and I was there entirely alone.

It was a pilgrimage I'd determined to make when I realized that Abu Simbel was within reach of Addis Ababa. The temple had been there since the 13th century B.C.; but it was in danger of being submerged by the lake that would form behind the Aswan Dam, then under construction. An international effort was about to begin to carve the temple into 20-ton blocks and reassemble it on higher ground. I wanted to see it in its last weeks in its original place.

I had flown from Addis to Khartoum and then taken an 18-hour trip by Sudanese Railways in a third-class carriage from Khartoum to Wadi Halfa, at the Egyptian border. I was in a compartment with a bunch of Sudanese who adopted me, gave me the place of honor to sleep (the luggage rack) and bought me pigeon and tea and cigarettes whenever we'd stop somewhere in the middle of the desert (or at least at places in the desert where we'd be surrounded by vendors waiting for the train). Then there was the boat trip from Wadi Halfa to Abu Simbel.

The statues of Ramses were astonishing, four of them, more than 60 feet from base to pharaonic double crown. The head of the statue second from the left had broken off, perhaps during a long-ago earthquake, and lay at Ramses's feet. Between the second and third statues was the entrance to a long hall leading to the inner chambers of the temple. If you were there on the right two mornings of the year, the rising sun would reach the sculptures on the far back wall of the final chamber.

I was carrying food and a sleeping bag that I rolled out that night next to Ramses's fallen head. At dawn (still entirely on my own), I sat and watched eastward across the Nile, waiting for the sun to rise. The statues of Ramses watched too, leaning slightly toward the coming dawn, and I could feel them relax and settle back as the sun crept above the horizon one more time.

Then there I was, still alone, with no idea when the next boat might come by to take me away again. I could see a shepherd far off in the distance, but there was no other sign of life. I just hung out with Ramses (who'd been there for 3,300 years and had learned patience along the way) as the day moved on.

Late in the afternoon, two tour boats appeared, coming south from the direction of Aswan. Tourists swarmed over the area, bands played, floodlights lit the statues – it was wild. I chatted with an Egyptian stewardess from one of the boats; she sneaked me on board, providing a place to sleep on the dining room floor. In the morning, as we were headed north along the Nile, I had breakfast with somebody from the British House of Lords. I have no idea what he made of me.

I got off in Aswan, found an Egyptian engineer who took me through the insides of the hydroelectric tunnels being constructed as part of the dam (climbing down the concave inside wall of a huge tunnel on spikes driven into the earth, backpack and sleeping bag swaying), then got on a boat headed back toward Sudan.

This time, the disreputable expatriates included a young man from the Netherlands. He was trying to win a bet that he could hitch-hike without money from the northern tip of Norway to the southern tip of Africa. He'd gotten as far as southern Egypt and had the rest of Africa to go. As the lot of us sat together in a cramped cabin, he explained very seriously that half his stomach had been shot away while he was part of a United Nations peacekeeping force in West Africa. If he didn't eat often, he said, he'd fart. We all shared our food with him.

Once in Sudan, he headed overland toward the Red Sea, planning to make his way down the coast to Massawa and then overland through Addis Ababa and southward. Weeks later, he appeared at my door in Addis, still broke, with an acute case of malaria. I nursed him back to health for a few days, gave him some food and money, took him to the edge of town and left him on the road to Nairobi. Even more weeks later, I got a postcard from him in Capetown; he'd won his bet.

For my part, once in Sudan I took another 18-hour train ride (in the course of which I got the worst food poisoning I've ever had), missed my plane from Khartoum, hitchhiked a ride on a US military plane to Asmara instead, then took a commercial flight back to Addis and my job.

TRAVELS WITH DAVID

Chapter 3

TRAVELS

1965-1980

Here is where my notes and journals fail me. I'll touch lightly on the high points, but you can skip ahead for travels that were better documented.

After two years in Ethiopia, I left in 1965 with Elena (a story to be told somewhere else), whom I'd first met while in Ethiopia in 1961. After I'd been a graduate student at Harvard University for two years, we married and moved to Lincoln University in Pennsylvania, where I taught economics and Elena taught African literature and French. Lincoln is a black university, and we found ourselves immersed in soul music and stories from our students that opened a window to the lives of African Americans in a sometimes overtly racist society. (One of my students was shot in the back by a policeman and killed while at home for Easter holidays. It would be nice to think that almost a half-century later things like that didn't happen anymore; but...) We were at our house near the campus when Martin Luther King was assassinated and immediately went to join the mourners, our whiteness standing out vividly through an evening of almost desperate emotion.

In 1978, we moved to Lagos, Nigeria, where I had a job with Arthur D. Little, a consulting firm advising the Federal Ministry of Industries on its industrial policies. There was a civil war going on in the east of the country, so there was nothing much happening, industrially speaking, to advise about. We traveled instead, driving to the country's northern territories (then much more peaceful than the south; now hotbeds of Islamic fundamentalism) and improvising business reasons to visit West African countries including Benin, Togo, Ghana, the Ivory Coast, and Senegal. We also joined my parents for a brief trip to East Africa.

Through the year in Nigeria, we acquired comfortable savings, mostly legitimately. (Again, there is a story here for another time.) Between June 1969 and August 1971, we travel binged, starting in Italy, watching the first moon landing with friends in Paris, living for a while in southern France, driving to Spain, flying back to the East Coast of the United States, and then traveling west to California. After time with friends in San Francisco, we settled for a few months in Santa Cruz, where Elena worked at a Polish-American restaurant and I drove a school bus.

I realized at the time that driving a bus is an excellent, compressed introduction to local culture. I kept noticing the process of socialization, the littlest kids bunching together and interacting with me and generally creating a noisy world of their own, the older kids spreading out and not looking at me, seeing the bus as just a transition between home and school. Watching them also gave insight into the world outside: a third-grade blonde girl to me as she gets off at her stop, "Those n---s won't keep quiet"; a third-grade black boy shouting out the window, "Goddamn cop"; another third-grader getting on with a happy, "Guess what, Mr. Bus Driver, my momma's got a new gun!"; the high school boy handing me a joint as he gets off the bus.

The littlest kids were the most disquieting. When the fever was upon them (and it was something that, unpredictably, swept through them like fire, past some subtle flash point or critical mass I didn't always see and couldn't always stop them short of), they could move anywhere. It involved self-destructive hysteria and a hint of mob violence. It would take little, I suspected, to have them diving out the windows of the bus, and I wondered what would happen if I chose a scapegoat and suggested they tear him to pieces.

I'd been working on my doctoral thesis, which was going to be about communal environments. When we heard of a promising urban commune in Portland, Oregon, we quit our jobs and moved there. It was an experience more illuminating than happy (I later recorded my impressions in an article in *The New York Times Magazine*); and after a couple of months, we drove back across the country to Vermont.

I said we were binge traveling during those years. Here's what I wrote in May 1971: "In the last 153 weeks (just about three years, or since Lincoln University), we have slept in 110 beds in 83 cities in 18 countries, a different city every 13 days (and a different bed every 10 days) for three years." We were more than ready to come to rest for a time.

In September 1971, we settled into jobs at Vermont's Johnson State College, largely to be near friends we'd made when we were teaching together at Lincoln University. We each taught half-time, collaborated on a book (*Working Communally*, about cooperative and communal groups, mostly in the United States, in the 19th and 20th centuries), and shared care of the newborn Tana.

In the summer of 1975, we flew to Rome to show Tana off to her grandparents there. We made a side trip to Florence, fell in love with a Donatello bas-relief in the church of Santa Croce, mailed our resignations to Johnson State, had a friend send us our stuff, and rented an apartment on the piazza by the church with the Donatello. The idea was to research and write about aspects of the social history of the Renaissance, but the grants that would have let us do that fell through, and in 1976 we tearfully said farewell to Florence and returned to the U.S.

We were in Washington, D.C., for the next four years. I worked first as a consultant to various foreign aid-related organizations and then took a job as the energy adviser to the Africa Bureau of the U.S. Agency for International Development. The high point of those years was the birth of Alex (then known as Sasha). I worked mostly in Washington but took the occasional brief trip to African countries including Niger, Senegal, and Lesotho.

TRAVELS WITH DAVID

Chapter 4
LIKUNI, MALAWI
1983

In 1980, we moved to Malawi, where I had a World Bank contract as Senior Energy Officer in the Ministry of Forestry and Natural Resources. My job was to create an Energy Studies Unit to do surveys of wood energy use, testing of technologies such as wood stoves and charcoal kilns, and analysis of the economics of reforestation. I supervised construction of headquarters for the ESU on the fringes of an agriculture college in Likuni, a 20-minute drive outside the capital, Lilongwe. In 1982, we moved into one of the staff houses I'd built a few minutes' walk from the new office. All the tales below of life there took place exactly as described. They didn't actually happen during the same week, but they might as well have.

SATURDAY

<u>1:30 a.m.</u> Dragged unwillingly from deepest sleep, I am once again made aware of how resonant and threatening Ringo's bark can be. This time it's one of our laborers with an urgent "complaint": his wife is very sick and needs the hospital. We drive several miles along an oxcart track to fetch her. Still three-quarters asleep, I feel us floating

15

down a tunnel of radiant greens, the maize rising above us and brushing the sides of the car. From time to time a village drifts by, its dark windowless back to us. Rats run under our wheels. When we arrive, the wife's sickness has just been purged in the form of a newborn son. Back home, and so to bed.

<u>8:00 a.m.</u> Roll out of bed and head for a reviving bath. There's nothing in the pipes but air. Lightning-quick, I deduce a relationship between the lack of water and the work that's been going on to re-lay our water lines. The basic insight accomplished, it's a mere two hours' work to locate the break and someone who can come fix it.

<u>11:30 a.m.</u> There's a three-mile stretch of road between us and anything paved. Returning from Tana's piano lesson, I hit an invisible mud slick and skid into the ditch. I stand in the muddy road, looking at the car and reflecting on how mornings like this fit into God's plan. Just then, the plumber drives by on his way to fix the water and gives me a cheery wave in passing. Tana and I walk the mile back to the house in something less than perfect spirits.

<u>5:00 p.m.</u> The watchman reports for duty with a long and barely comprehensible tale of woe. It all has to do with his baby's illness, which somehow required a trip to his village by his wife (and possibly himself or the baby), returning from which the wife (or the baby, or both) got lost, requiring an extensive hunt by the watchman, who ultimately found somebody, although somebody else may still be missing. One thing I do understand: this cost a lot of money, so could he borrow ten kwacha?

<u>10:30 p.m.</u> It is one of those electric nights when the drums *start* agitated and screw the pitch up steadily from there. The drumming and the songs and the shrieks drift across the dambo from the village just down the Likuni Mission road. The Gule Wamkulu[1] dance down the road covered in maize husks and feathers, shouting out things that make the flesh crawl even when you can't understand them. All the world's dogs join in, seemingly hundreds of them in hearing range.

---

[1] A secret society among the Chewa people in the region.

The dog nearest by is possessed: it keeps up a steady, sharp four barks a second and can obviously go on forever. We sleep restlessly, or not at all. After several hours, on some abrupt signal inaudible to us, everything – drums, dogs, singers – hits a beat and simultaneously stops dead. The world unfolds into utter silence, and finally we sleep.

SUNDAY

8:30 a.m. There's cold water in the house, but no hot. Yesterday's repairs filled the line with dirt, which has now plugged the valve at the hot water holding tank. We haven't a ladder, so I climb the shelves in the shed to get to the tank. We lack the proper tools, so I clamp a wrench to the pipe and beat it with a hammer to get at the valve. The procedure is crude, and so are my reflections. Eventually, we have hot water.

10:00 a.m. Earnest's dog is at our end of the compound again. Ernest is the ESU's surveys officer. He and his family somehow survive on a tiny government salary, and I sometimes wonder how many crumbs from his table he's able to save for the dog. Not many, I imagine, since his dog comes over to our place and eats Ringo's shit. I don't want to think too much about this…

2:00 p.m. Our gardener is back from leave. He brought with him a "brother" (nephew) and a "sister" (niece), both now in school in town. They came into his charge shortly after he got home, when his sister (sister?) and her husband died after being poisoned by a traditional doctor. In the aftermath, the neighbors came and stripped the house bare of everything of value. So, could he borrow a month's salary to cover school fees?

3:30 p.m. We're driving to a colleague's place for tea. A man on a bicycle zips out from a side street, sees us, panics, wobbles, tips over and slides across the road in front of the car. We flatten one of his tires but unaccountably miss any part of him. I drop off Elena and the children and head for the police station, where statements are taken. I'm just finishing when the investigating officer is called away for a moment.

An hour later, I'm still sitting there swapping stories with the bicyclist and several of his friends.

11:00 p.m. A hyena is prowling our fence line, daring Ringo to come out and mix it up a bit. It may be the one that got some of our neighbor's chickens a couple of nights ago. We lie in bed wondering if the gate is closed. Eventually the hyena wanders off into the night, cooing mildly – and deceptively – as it goes.

MONDAY

7:30 a.m. I am walking to work down the narrow dirt lanes that pass for roads in our area. The sun is shining through the most brilliant and fragrant air I know. These days, the maize reaches above my head, the grass is at knee level, the trees are bushy and dense. The whole world seems green and moist; and if you let your mind wander, the feeling comes upon you that you are walking under water. In the field across from my office, a dozen snow-white egrets browse among the cows.

7:45 a.m. It is a morning for heavy logistics. My accountant, Mr. Mkoola, needs to collect everyone's wages at the bank. The typist, Mrs. Mabaso, needs an injection at the hospital. The Land Rover has broken a bolt – apparently the one that connects the rear wheels to the chassis – and needs service. My Systems Testing Officer, Justin Manong'a, is headed for Bunda College to measure the calorific value of our charcoal samples. Mr. Yokoniya, the messenger, needs maize flour. We are supposed to pick up 250 leucaena tree seedlings for our agroforestry trial. Earnest needs to duplicate more answer sheets for the urban energy survey. The country ran out of petrol ten days ago, and our tanks are all but empty. Hello, Monday.

9:00 a.m. For several days, Mr. Charm the charcoaler labored to erect an earth-mound kiln behind the workshop. Each piece of wood was weighed and the various stages of construction timed. In a hurry for results, we fired the kiln yesterday, and Mr. Charm sat all night by it to tend its needs. Now is the critical moment in the process – and a torrential rain has begun to fall, soaking the earth and extinguishing the wood. I guess next week we try again.

10:15 a.m. I call our building contractor to discuss current events. The men re-laying the pipes to our house are doing rotten work. Only a trickle of hot water gets to the bathtub. Every time the pressure drops and is restored, the water turns a chocolate brown. I've provided Mr. Mkoola with a staff house nearby, but its roof leaks. The contractor will immediately put his best men to work on all these problems. Why am I not reassured?

12:15 p.m. Lunchtime. Elena is describing the morning's drive to school. Sitting in the middle of the Lilongwe road was a little girl, perhaps five years old. Dressed only in a tattered bathrobe, she rocked back and forth to some inner dissonance of her own. When Elena stopped, a demented Brit zipped by in his Land Rover and nearly killed them all. Malawians walked by with curious looks, but nobody thought to help. Finally, Elena got the girl on her feet and walking toward what appeared to be her village.

1:45 p.m. The Chief Forestry Officer is careening through space. He wants us to build a charcoal kiln as big as The Ritz. This would demonstrate our ability to substitute charcoal for the coal now being used by a number of companies here. I quote the ESU's charcoal study, which estimated that such a plan would cost $10.5 million in subsidies, money that the Government doesn't have. He looks at me as if I were speaking Xhosa and goes on planning the kiln.

2:30 p.m. We have a team of enumerators, who ask respondents our questions when we carry out a survey. Earnest and I are talking with them about Mzuzu, where they've just done our urban energy survey. They explain that people don't pay much for wood there. Why? It's a matter of local custom. Most people have a friend who works for the government, and they take turns running their office Land Rovers out to the forest reserve to collect the wood and carry it back home. The enumerators see the look on my face and burst out laughing. Me, I'm just trying to imagine how we're going to report this particular survey finding.

10:15 p.m. The cat is in heat. She prowls outside the house with her boyfriends, or in search of them, yowling horribly. It's a sound that a million years of evolution have fine-tuned to rouse her boyfriends to uncontrollable lust and her owners to uncontrollable rage. We try to lure her inside so we can drown her, but she eludes us and continues the prowl.

TUESDAY

8:00 a.m. There was a storm last night, and lightning took out the phone extension to our house. Trying to ring us from the office, Mrs. Mabaso discovers we've been cut off and reports the problem to Telephone Faults. It's a welcome initiative on her part, except that the faults office sucks up complaints like quicksand. I would have called the regional engineer directly, but I decide to wait until tomorrow and resign myself to a couple of days without a phone.

8:30 a.m. Justin fires up the brick charcoal kiln. It cracks on all four sides and the wood burns to ash. We arrange to have the kiln rebuilt.

9:45 a.m. The Chief Forestry Officer is tumbling out of control. He has decided he needs a massive study, using satellite imagery and "ground truth" field investigations, to count Malawi's trees, village by village. He then wants to measure the consumption of wood, house by house. With sophisticated map overlays and computer printouts, he will then be able to determine where wood is scarce, area by area. I suggest we just go to villagers and *ask* if wood is scarce; we have found they usually know. He looks at me as if I were speaking Cantonese and goes on planning his study.

11:00 a.m. The plumber has come to supervise the pipe laying and to fix Mr. Mkoola's roof. Unfortunately, he forgot his ladder, so the roof will have to wait until tomorrow. While he is sitting in front of the office playing a game of bawo with my driver, one of the work crew puts his pick through the water line. The water is off for the rest of the day while repairs are made.

<u>2:00 p.m.</u> The phone is working again. What does Mrs. Mabaso know that I don't know?

<u>2:45 p.m.</u> Earnest and I are searching for one of the wood energy nurseries to try out our seedling sales questionnaire. Just now, we're driving down a nonexistent track, the car parting grass almost as high as the windows. In every direction, the hills and the maize and the mango trees roll out to a vast horizon. If he were painting this, Leonardo would have to re-think his attitude toward atmospheric perspective – the air is so intensely clear that there is no such thing. Objects far out there are as vivid and as crisply defined as objects right here. So much of the world is *present* that I find myself getting dizzy from the overload.

<u>3:30 p.m.</u> We've found the nursery. From nowhere, the clouds have gathered and it has begun gently to rain. We talk with the nurseryman, surrounded by ranked armies of tree seedlings – gmelina, leucaena, eucalyptus, cassia. Our project lives or dies in nurseries like this. There are 82 of them around the country, each ready to sell 100,000 seedlings a year to help farmers meet their fuelwood needs. The nurseryman unfolds his story: the district forester ran out of supplies, so most of the nursery's seed was inferior stock collected from under nearby trees, so most of the seedlings died; anyway, he only sold 2,500 seedlings this year, 2,000 of them to a grocer who's going to make a killing selling the trees for building poles; of course, those are only estimates, since he ran out of receipt books three weeks ago and nobody has replaced them; not only that, but… We finally leave, chilled by what I suppose is the rain.

<u>5:30 p.m.</u> After weeks of preparation, we finally collect Tana and Alex's lambs. We have their bags of maize husks (bartered from villagers nearby in exchange for salt), their feeding bottles, and a place for them to stay in the pen with the chickens. Judging by their apparent intelligence, they and the chickens should relate as equals. From the bleating and cackling that's gone on out there since they came, they seem to be getting on fine. Don't want to think how *we* will get on, having added yet a new commotion to the usual nighttime howlings and yowlings and cooings of dogs, cats, owls, hyenas…

9:45 p.m. Bedtime. Checking the house, we find the watchman asleep on our porch. He proves difficult to waken, sunk as he is in a drunken coma. We finally stand him up, and he staggers away into the trees.

WEDNESDAY

5:15 a.m. The lambs are up and so is Elena, trying to feed them. They refuse to eat and bleat piteously for their mother. Eventually they have everyone up and sympathizing with them in varying degrees, me least of all.

8:15 a.m. Now the extension to our house works only when the sun is out. When it begins to rain, the phone goes dead. Since this is the rainy season, we have a problem. Mrs. Mabaso makes her report to Telephone Faults.

10:00 a.m. The Chief Forestry Officer is sending off sparks. An EEC[2] delegation has arrived with bags of money they want to spend on wood energy "microprojects." All Malawi has to do is pay half the cost. I remind him that all the activities now worth doing are already covered by our World Bank project, under which we pay only 25% of costs. Any shift of activities to EEC financing will therefore double what Malawi has to pay. He looks at me as if I were speaking Chichewa and hurries after the delegation with a fistful of proposals.

11:15 a.m. The plumber brought his ladder to check Mr. Mkoola's roof, but he forgot the materials to make the repair. I put him to work instead cleaning out our hot water valve, which is plugged again from yesterday's adventures with the water line.

2:30 p.m. The enumerators have uncovered the Land Rover effect right here in Lilongwe. In one of their interviews, a Mrs. Kasinje reported that all her wood comes 25 miles from our project's fuelwood plantation, fetched by her husband in his department's Land Rover. How can that be, I ask. The enumerators have a most amazing coincidence to report: Mrs. Kasinje's husband is Mr. Kasinje, our project's executive officer. Here's one survey finding we won't even try to report.

---

[2]The European Economic Community, later the European Union.

2:45 p.m. While we talk, our own Land Rover is sitting outside the office window. Apparently finding the conversation offensive, it bursts into flames. We put it out.

4:00 p.m. The repairman has been here to fix our phone. Unfortunately, it was sunny when he came, the phone was working fine, and he found no problem. He suggests we ring him the next time it rains. I ponder that one, and he heads back to town. Ten minutes later it starts to rain, and the phone goes dead. Now what?

5:30 p.m. Mr. Mkoola lingers after work. The country being out of petrol, he wants to buy some of the ESU reserve for his motorcycle. I am reluctant until he explains the situation: his wife is very pregnant, and he may need to rush her to Likuni Mission Hospital. I pour the petrol, all the while imagining a stormy night, the three miles of rutted muddy road, Mrs. Mkoola in some late stage of labor, the motorcycle...

10:30 p.m. There's a new night bird here on migration from some unusually disordered province of Albania. The bird produces a series of piercing, rising whistles, each starting at a slightly higher pitch and anxiety level than the one before. It's a little like the alarm that tells you your submarine is sinking, only more shattering. The first time it woke us up, I was on my feet before I realized what was going on. And just when we'd gotten used to the unknown creatures who swoop at the windows in the night, shrieking as they come...

THURSDAY

5:15 a.m. The lambs are up early again, along with Elena and Alex; Tana follows not long after. I wedge pillows around my head and sleep for another hour. By the time I get up, nobody is speaking to anybody else. For their part, the lambs bleat on.

7:45 a.m. A spot of trouble at the office. One of the students at the college nearby came over earlier and made a rather explicit proposal to the watchman's wife. Unfortunately, the watchman was there and didn't like what he was hearing. Now the watchman is missing two teeth and the student needs stitches in his head. The vice-principal of the college piles them into a van and sets off on the police/hospital run.

<u>8:45 a.m.</u> The water crew is driving me crazy, and it's my own fault. Several weeks ago, I discovered they had buried the line at a depth of eight inches instead of the specified three feet. Being compulsive, I insisted they dig it up and do the job right. Why didn't I just forget it? Now, the crew has dug up a section of pipe with four leaky joints. The water is off for the rest of the day while repairs are made. Under the circumstances, of course, nothing can be done about Mr. Mkoola's roof.

<u>11:00 a.m.</u> The Chief Forestry Officer is bouncing off the walls. It has come upon him to install a fuelwood plantation on Likoma Island, near the Mozambique coast on the other side of Lake Malawi. This would serve as a model for a national program to provide farmers with the wood they're not growing fast enough themselves. I do some fast calculations and discover that such a program would cost about $100 million a year, or one-third of the national budget. Perhaps, I say, we should look for another idea. He looks at me as if I were speaking Urdu and goes on planning his project.

<u>1:45 p.m.</u> There's a great commotion outside, workers throwing stones at something on the roadside. By the time I get there, it's a fairly battered snake, perhaps three feet long. It's an ndala, I'm told, and absolutely lethal. None of our dictionaries reveal what an ndala is in English, but I'll be just as happy not to see another one.

<u>3:30 p.m.</u> Outside my window, a man with a leaky hose in his hand and a rusty tank on his back is spraying the grass. What with? – he doesn't know. I find his supervisor, who knows only that the spray is supposed to kill termites. I ring the suppliers in Blantyre, who say the stuff is Aldrin. Aldrin is so unbelievably nasty that practically every country in the world now bans it outright. It kills in seven different ways, quick and slow, and can be breathed, swallowed, or just absorbed through the skin. Outside my window, the man with the tank

is walking barefoot through the grass he's just sprayed. The rest of the afternoon is spent in an impromptu Aldrin education campaign.

<u>5.45 p.m.</u> The end of the workday at last. I lock up the office, turn to walk home, and freeze. Surely a hallucination has come upon the world. As far as can be seen, one quadrant of the sky is a clenched purple black, the kind of deadly panorama that would have panicked God into creating light. The gigantic streaks of lightning cutting the dark only emphasize its starkness and foreboding. Next to this is a quadrant of sky all golden and peach and steaming clouds, the sun poised just above a horizon of far-off purple hills. On this side, the jacaranda trees are backlit in a way that makes them seem on fire, and a thousand watery diamonds cling to the fence across the road. Even the maize plants are radiating a celestial light. Next comes a quadrant all summery afternoon, pastel sky and pastel clouds. The last quadrant seems somehow empty, except for the grandest rainbow I have ever seen. It towers through the void to the top of the sky, one foot in dreamy afternoon and one foot in the storm.

<u>6:30 p.m.</u> Alex and Tana are exploring some new game. "We should get Papa to play," says Alex. Tana laughs. "We'll have to wait until he's more frisky," she says. "These days he just sits around with a headache and complains about the Chief Forestry Officer!" Oh, God…

<u>8:30 p.m.</u> Father Michael is over for the evening, and we're having dinner. There is suddenly chaos outside; Ringo is obviously trying to disembowel an intruder. It turns out to be Mr. Yokoniya, whose wife has apparently been in labor since the previous night. We make it to the hospital before the baby appears, and I stop trying to remember whether you're supposed to cut the cord or leave it alone.

FRIDAY

<u>4:00 a.m.</u> Ringo again: there's some ruckus up at Justin's house. It appears the watchmen have come to report a drunk at the office, someone insisting the doors be unlocked so he can find a place to sleep. The

watchmen didn't like the man's attitude, so they beat him for a while and then came to Justin for further instructions. Justin investigates, rids us of the drunk, and we all head back to bed.

<u>7:45 a.m.</u> All three office phones are out, along with the extension to our house. Also, the switchboard hasn't been working properly, but that hasn't seemed critical since the lines have been so faulty anyway. This time I go see the telephone engineer himself so we can speculate together on why we're having all these troubles. He promises to send his best men to work on the problem. Why am I not reassured?

<u>9:00 a.m.</u> The plumber finally remembered to bring both the ladder and the materials to work on Mr. Mkoola's roof. However, after considering the problem, he looks regretful: "Sorry, it's not raining now, so I can't find the leak to fix it." Just then it begins to rain, and I note our good fortune. The plumber looks at me disdainfully: "Ah, but I can't fix the roof when it's *raining*!" I'm heading back to the office to call the contractor when I remember we have no phones.

<u>10:15 a.m.</u> The contractor arrives as I'm about to leave for a meeting. We've been exchanging frank words over the phone about his company's work, so I stay to patch things up. We walk the water line, discussing the different kinds of leaks we find. We try in vain to imagine why the water turns brown every time the pressure drops. We puzzle over the mystery of the hot water that doesn't reach the bathtub. We commiserate with each other about Mr. Mkoola's roof. Then we have a Coke and he tells me about his home leave in Portugal, his lawsuits, his wife's Jaguar, and his admiration for President Reagan ("At last, America's fighting back"). The morning is ebbing away as we part, the best of friends. Only, the pipes and the roof still leak, the water is still brown, the hot water still doesn't get to the tub, and I've missed the meeting. Also, my head hurts.

<u>1:15 p.m.</u> Payday was four days ago, and all the enumerators came to pay off the interest-free loans I provide in time of need. This afternoon they're all back with assorted problems: my sister needs school fees, I need to buy flour, thieves stole my money, my uncle died, my brother's

in jail, can you lend me ten kwacha. I ask businesslike questions, surrender, and say yes to everybody. Next month, I tell myself for the twentieth time, this will have to stop.

<u>2:00 p.m.</u> The new brick kiln is dry and ready for testing. Justin fires it up. It cracks on all four sides and the wood burns to ash.

<u>2:30 p.m.</u> Mr. Mkoola announces that our gardener has been at his house to sell a couple of used motorcycle tires. Might they be ours? I head for home. Sure enough, the tires are not in their place in the shed. The gardener is absolutely astonished at their absence. He wanders around the compound, looking to see if possibly they've been mislaid in the chicken coop or on the roof. I decide to become invisible, on the theory the tires will then be discovered "in the bush" and we can manage not to fire him. Time goes by, then the gardener appears – sure enough, the tires have been discovered in the bush.

<u>4:00 p.m.</u> The Chief Forestry Officer is spinning like a pinwheel. I have asked for a contract extension, and he has decided this means dealing with three related questions first. In a matter of moments, he has the Secretary for Personnel Management on one line, the Chairman of the Public Service Commission on another, and his Principal Personnel Officer standing by to give advice. I can't follow all the things that happen next, but he finally hangs up, triumphant. Now there are *six* questions to be dealt with before considering my extension. With a sinking feeling, I recognize my position: we're well into the countdown to end of contract (seven months, six months, five months…), and it's résumé time again. Damn, damn, damn.[3]

<u>6:00 p.m.</u> Elena has set Chopin aside and is filling the house with Scott Joplin. Even on our battered and out-of-tune piano, the music gladdens the spirit. Tana is reading to Alex in his tub, though there's constant punctuation by laughter and stories of their own. (Alex was earlier in the household staff quarters, to which the gardener and his

---

[3]The contract extension finally came through, and we had another year in Likuni much the same as the week described here.

girlfriend had retreated, and could hardly wait to get Tana to himself to describe whatever it was he found there.) The cats and dog and lambs are peacefully eating dinner. I distrust moments like this; they deceive you into thinking that life is under control, and then...

10:00 p.m. The watchman who borrowed ten kwacha last weekend is back. He looks small and frightened. His sick baby was ultimately taken to Likuni Hospital, where it has just died. He needs to get the body, his wife, and her relatives back to their village. We go find my driver and the Land Rover, and I send them all off into the dark, dark night.

Chapter 5

NEPAL

MAY 1986

In October 1984, we moved to Rome, where I carried out consultancies for organizations including the World Bank, the International Fund for Agricultural Development, the Food and Agriculture Organization, the International Labor Organization, the World Resources Institute, and the Beijer Institute. For my work, I traveled to countries ranging from Lesotho to Bangladesh. In one consultancy with FAO, I worked with local experts and government officials in Nepal to create a system for adding socioeconomic information to watershed planning.

Kathmandu is an enchanted city. It is compact and complex and various, and a lot of the complexity is decorative, little patches of color patted together on buses, rickshaws, buildings, trucks, temples. There are cows lying contemplatively in the streets and herds of goats by the post office. The streets are mostly narrow, and the sidewalks narrower, so people watching you go by from the second-story windows are within easy chatting distance – if you can chat in Nepalese. Traffic teems and seems to be mostly bicycles, an astonishing variety of three-wheeled vehicles (pushed, pedaled, or motor-driven), and the oldest buses in the world.

*   *   *

I'm here to help the government put together a survey instrument to find how farmers manage their land and think about watershed issues. Pyakuryal is a local sociologist who's been hired to help, along with Sthaphit, representing the Department of Watershed Management. They and I spend all day in Kavre District looking at the ways land is now being used, finding out from Sthaphit how the project thinks it *should* be used if the watersheds are to survive, and speculating about the social and economic issues that arise in trying to get the project's ideas implemented. We'll make a tentative list of those issues, followed by a description of the information needed to understand them and a questionnaire designed to gather the information. Then we'll go back and ask the questions of farmers and see what happens.

It is a grueling process. I am at once student and teacher, but I am in control of both roles, selecting what I need to learn and teach. The work is incessant – if I blank out, everyone else settles back meditatively and nothing happens. Even when I'm trying to find things out, I have to explain somehow why these are important things, not just idle curiosity, so that the process of taking farmers seriously (not just as objects of government instructions) begins to grow clear.

*   *   *

Pyakuryal has good headquarters-field stories. When he was an extension agent, he put some demonstration areas out in the hills to reach people who never made it to the main road. The next time the headquarters types came calling in their Land Rover, they gave him hell because they couldn't get to the areas and back to town in time for dinner. All this was contrary to accepted demonstration practice, they said. The next year, Pyakuryal put two or three demonstration areas on the main road, and everyone was happy.

We're on that kind of a field trip today – far enough to feel we've been in the bush, near enough to be back at the International Club by dinnertime. Mostly we are looking at landslides, accompanied by Signore Gregori, an FAO landslide consultant. (This trip has been almost worth it just to learn that there are such things as landslide consultants.) Looking around, Gregori shakes his head. "Queste frane," he says, "un brutto problema." ("These landslides, an ugly problem.") He speaks as much English as I speak Italian, but perhaps you can't be picky when choosing landslide consultants.

Also with us is P.K. Mool, Nepal's own landslide expert. Explaining how some of the vegetation works, Mool tells us this story:

> One spring high in the hills of Nepal, the Rhododendron was bursting with bloom and beauty. A nearby Nepalese Alder fell in love with her and proposed marriage. But the Alder is bare and scraggly in the spring, and the Rhododendron refused him, laughing at his ugliness. At this, the Alder threw himself to his death down the mountainside. And this is why in Nepal the Rhododendron lives high in the hills, while the Nepalese Alder is found lower down, especially at the bottom of landslides.

*　　　　　*　　　　　*

The Nepalese hills are extraordinary. We climb from Kathmandu's 4,000 feet to 6,500 feet or so (leaving us 23,000 feet below Everest, not far away). Even here, the terrain is rugged enough – the little kids are like their Ethiopian counterparts in being absolutely sure-footed on the narrow paths, while I slip and slide. *Everything* is terraced, either flat for rice paddy or sloping gently for maize and other crops. The terraces hang almost over the road – some are no more than two feet by four, tucked into a space between field and midair. Grasses are planted along the terrace risers and then used to feed livestock, whose manure is composted and put on the fields.

The system grows more precarious all the time: population pressure is pushing crops farther up the hillsides to nearly unreachable land, soils (and sometime whole hillsides) are washing away, and overall productivity is falling. And yet, so much care is going into the ways land is used that almost everything is being done right already. What else is there to do? The government has its ideas; our surveys should help tell whether it's on the right track.

*   *   *

A Sunday morning and off to church. Inculturation: most people take off their shoes and sit in meditation poses (or at least cross-legged) on cushions on the floor. The Nepalese priest sits behind the altar throughout the service, except for reading of the gospel, homily, and communion. For hymns, a guitar is supplemented by tabla and temple bells. When we give each other the sign of peace, it is with hands together, fingertips to forehead in the Hindu manner. And yet the mysteries are the same: I am not worthy to receive you, Lord, but only say the word and I shall be healed.

Driving back to the hotel, the driver wants to know where I come from. Italy, I say. Ah yes, Italy, he says, is that a Christian country? I think I must be a long way from home.

*   *   *

Back from another day in Kavre District. I am sufficiently mellowed (or stunned) that I don't push these days much. I'm remembering why civil servants like field trips (not even counting the profit you make on your per diem when you're away overnight): you don't work very hard, you usually pass a market or a horticultural center where you can buy things more cheaply than in town, and you spend a lot of your time sitting blanked-out in the Land Rover, just letting things pass by. Much nicer than almost any of the things that go on in offices.

This time B.D. Shrestha came with Pyakuryal and me. Shrestha is a geologist who did his advanced training in the Netherlands. I try to imagine all the similarities between the geology of Nepal and the geology of Holland, but it doesn't come easy.

*   *   *

With a morning free, I go to Bodhnath. Following a narrow road off the square, I splash through rain and the kind of urban mud that would keep a high school biology lab guessing for years at what they were seeing in their microscopes. Several hundred yards on is a monastery under construction, a rectangle of tiny cells around a great, enclosed shrine to the Buddha.

I enter the shrine itself, a huge room occupied by a half-dozen sculptors working on the great Buddha at the center of the front wall. The Buddha (missing his head and hands still) is perhaps ten feet tall from thigh to where his head will be. He is flanked on each side by a great deer standing on a tiger standing on an elephant. Above his head is a dark demon with snakes coming from its mouth. In profusion all around are maidens, flowers, dragons, snakes in vivid oranges, blues, scarlets, golds, pinks – a riot of color and energy. In the midst of this is the Buddha, absolutely serene even in his unfinished state.

A half-dozen sculptors are at work. Three young men on precarious scaffolding are smoothing the clay of the Buddha's chest and arms. They work in complete silence, curved wooden tools passing over the chest, around his nipples, smoothing him down to skin and muscle. In a corner of the room, a boy sits astride a length of timber, smoothing and smoothing the fingers of the Buddha's detached hands. I watch for a few minutes, then catch the boy's eye and gesture with my camera: May I take a picture? The boy smiles and nods. The flash and the click of the shutter are muted by the silence.

Alone in the rear of the room, the master artist – all wrinkles and rheumy eyes and wispy white hair – sits cross-legged on scaffolding raised several feet off the floor. Spread over a wire frame in front of him is the missing face of the Buddha, emerging from clay under the man's knotted hands. Perhaps half-finished, the face is already radiant with repose and power. In absolute concentration, the old man is caressing into being the Buddha's brow, his cheeks. I raise my camera and again snap the shutter.

In that moment, the nearer half of the Buddha's head begins slowly to slide off its frame. Puzzled, the old man reaches out for the sagging face, as one would reach to catch a falling child. The rest of the clay begins to collapse then, the man tenderly hugging the face to his chest in an instinctive attempt to keep the Buddha whole. His apprentices come running, the scaffolding is surrounded by them now, a ring of silent concentration on the broken Buddha.

*   *   *

There is a kind of Land Rover culture that prevails when the expat settles back out of sight during field trips and lets things find their way. The Land Rover stops and starts in unpredictable rhythms. People get out and disappear, while those who stay behind sit quietly and patiently. Still other people appear and get in, upon which the Land Rover sets off at right angles to its expected course. Then it stops and everyone gets out. And so on. Eventually, you end up back at the point where all this started, the right people present in the right numbers, heading in a direction that makes sense, but with no idea what has happened along the way.

*   *   *

We are trekking today, about five hours up into the mountains and three hours back down again, stopping along the way to talk with people or look at some kind of conservation work. All along the way, we pass hill people bringing potatoes and ghee down to market or paraffin and salt back up again. The loads rest low on the back, supported by a strap that loops around the forehead, and everybody is hauling weight that I could manage only on level ground.

It is a trekkers' route, so there are periodic teahouses with Coke and Fanta and Lemu. The houses are more sturdy and more often tin-roofed than average, since this is the "main road" to somewhere and people profit from the trade and the access to town. Still, the essentials can't have changed much – the buffalo lying on the porch and the goats in the door descend from other buffalo and goats that have hung out in the same places for generations.

We meet the project's favorite farmer, the one that always gets trotted out to tell visitors how wonderful the project is. This year, the project paid him to level-terrace and protect some of his land. In an area where every inch of ground is cultivated, however, I can't help noticing that his new terraces are all fallow. Then the Swiss fodder expert who came with us explains that this farmer has borrowed large amounts of money from the Agricultural Development Bank, done nothing agricultural, and never repaid it. He seems to have figured out the system: everybody gives him money, and he keeps it. FAO, the Department of Watershed Management, and the Favorite Farmer form a perfect whole; all he has to do is give an occasional rap on ecology for passing development tourists, and the system is maintained.

*   *   *

After our second interview with a farmer (we're pretesting the survey), I get us talking about what we've found out. According to Shrestha, the farmer's land is seriously erosion-prone and should immediately be level-terraced, with stone waterways to prevent gullying. Otherwise, the productivity of the land will continue to fall. But (note I) the farmer told us that he doesn't now *have* an erosion problem and that because of chemical fertilizers the land's productivity is *increasing*; given these beliefs, is he likely to be highly motivated to put large amounts of labor into level-terracing? Well, maybe not (says Shrestha), but we might suggest he take the land out of crops and put it into fruit trees instead. Okay (say I), but he told us he already has too little land to grow the food his family needs; is he likely to be interested in taking land out of food production? Well, maybe not (say Shrestha), but then the project should provide incentives. What kind of incentives (ask I)? And so it goes. Supposing our survey *does* find out what farmers are up to and want, would the government be able to absorb the information?

I sometimes feel like an interpreter, trying to find some way to let farmer and technician communicate across a great cultural divide. For example, the technician worries about erosion; the farmer thinks about what his land produces. If fertilizer raises output even while soil is washing away, what do the two people have in common to talk about? It's my job to help them talk. I only wish the government's immediate response to "Here's what the farmer is saying" would not always be "Well then, we'll provide him incentives to change his mind."

It gets worse – all the folks thinking of things the farmers should do have such different professional perspectives. The watershed people want trees and grasses growing to save the soil, which means keeping the animals out; the livestock people want water for animals to drink and agricultural wastes for them to eat, and don't much worry about what the animals do to the soils; the horticulturalists want fruit for farmers' incomes, which means *not* planting the trees on the fragile slopes where they would hold the land but produce little fruit, and on and on. All these people are "collaborating" on the development of the watershed, but their realities are different from each other – and *all* differ from what the farmer lives. How can it possibly work?

*   *   *

Some weeks later, I return to Nepal to finish my consultancy. I'll produce a report, but without a great deal of hope for its successful implementation. When I have a morning off, I arrange once more to be dropped at Bodhnath, then retrace my steps through the network of paths to the monastery. I'm carrying two photos. One shows a young boy working with a wooden tool to smooth the lines of a disembodied hand. The other is of an old man, under whose hands a powerful face is forming.

A passing monk looks at the photos, disappears into one of the cells, and re-emerges with the boy. The boy has a smile as warm and open now as it had been when I inquired about taking his picture. He takes the photo and examines it at length. It occurs to me that it may be the first photo of himself he has ever seen.

The boy looks for a moment at the other photo and then leads me down the block of cells. In one of the rooms, an old man in an undershirt and tattered shorts is heating water on a tiny electric ring. He comes to the door and looks at me blankly. I think, how much smaller he seems without his clay.

I hand the old man the second photo. He looks at it curiously for a few moments, then sees who it is. His whole face wrinkles into a happy, toothless smile. He says a word or two I don't understand and then goes back to his picture. As I walk away down the path to Bodhnath, he is still looking at the photo and smiling, smiling.

*   *   *

"Consultancy"

At first is opening, and taking in;
near pain, so much openness –
you hope the things that enter
will have grace.
But then comes closing on those things,
a feeling of their form,
and this is the fragile time:
closing well enough to shape
but not to interrupt,
the things and you together
making birth.

TRAVELS WITH DAVID

Chapter 6
ETHIOPIA
MAY-JUNE 1987[4]

From September 1986 until April 1995, I worked for the United Nations World Food Program in Rome. I served as the natural resources expert in a small group of specialists whose job it was to look at WFP development activities with a professional eye. The best part of the job was when I got to travel to other countries, usually working with a small team to evaluate a WFP project. The entries that follow record short-term visits to Ethiopia, India, Vietnam, and Sudan.

The doors of the airplane swing open to the familiar smells of Addis Ababa: piss, berbere, and eucalyptus smoke. I take a deep breath, and am happy.

At the beginning of the 20th century, the emperor Menelik brought eucalypts from Australia to reforest a largely bare countryside. Everywhere now, people cook injera with the eucalypts' leaves and heat homes with their wood. Pervasive as air, the pungent smoke works its way down into your brain stem. At that point, you scarcely smell the stuff; it instead becomes the ground across which all of life here is played out.

I am in Ethiopia to look at the World Food Program's watershed management projects. One reason the place is so vulnerable to famine

---

[4]Published in edited form (under the pen name "Douglas Stevens") as "Ethiopian Landscapes," in *Commonweal*, November 20, 1987

is that soils are everywhere washing away. When the rains don't come, or when they come too fast, the thin soils cannot hold the crops. Working through the Ministry of Agriculture, we give food to farmers as payment to plant trees, build soil bunds and terraces, anything that will renew and stabilize the soil.

You've got to be impressed by how much our projects have gotten done; everybody says that. Mile after mile, there are terraces, bunds, woodlots, regenerated hillsides. When you look closely, you see the flaws – bunds broken, great gaps where the trees have died – but how very much work has visibly gone into it. It makes me think of technologies like the space shuttle – look at what we can do! – but what can we expect to come of it?

*　　　　　*　　　　　*

We are driving to Dessie, in the heart of Wollo Province. This is the region where the BBC took all those films of starving children during the terrible drought of 1984. There was a phenomenon in Wollo then called "closing the house": families would tidy up their affairs, sit down together, and die. Now, hillsides are everywhere green. Patches of rich, freshly-plowed earth alternate with patches of crops ready for harvest after the short rains. In some places, people didn't even bother to plant their short-rains crops, preferring to catch up on marriages and memorial services instead. They will regret this, since the big rains are about to fail again; but nobody knows that yet.

Halfway to Dessie, the road winds down off the high central plateau in order to move north through the Rift Valley. Just before, at Tarma Ber, the road swings out to the very lip of the plateau. Eagles hang motionless in mid-air here, resting on the winds sweeping up the mountain's face. Below them, through a great cut in the mountainside, you look down at the valley far below.

When I was here many years ago, during Emperor Haile Selassie's reign, I was struck by the beauty of that valley: it was as if God had flung down a great handful of mud houses and gardens and people, scattering them through the Rift. There was disorder there, and complete harmony. In 1974, though, the emperor was overthrown by a

Marxist military junta, the "Derg." As one means of reorganizing society along more "rational" grounds, the Derg forced rural people into newly-created villages, their houses lined up in neat rows like military barracks. "Villagization" did away with the disorder of rural life – and destroyed its harmony.

There is a rationale for this. If people are gathered from scattered farms and grouped in villages, the government can more easily give them drinking water, schools, and clinics – or so goes the theory. But grouping farmers (at their own expense) has proved easier than providing them with services (which often never come). Villages are choked with dust in the dry season and mud in the wet, and epidemics sweep freely through the crowds. Some people like the result anyway, especially the young, who enjoy the villages' open social life. Others are less happy, finding themselves jammed together with people they don't like. But villagization is a blunt instrument; when it strikes, *everybody* moves, the happy and the sad.

This is no small upheaval. The Ethiopian Airlines calendar for 1987 has sketches and descriptions of traditional houses from various parts of the country. (March: "The Oromo people live in round houses built of locally available materials – wood or bamboo – and are thatched.") I am told the calendar will become a collector's item. Given the pace of villagization, there soon won't *be* any traditional housing in Ethiopia. Can a change this fundamental really be sustained?

I wonder the same about these vast projects we are seeing. At one point, I stand at the end of a bridge on the Gondar road, looking at the terraced hillside opposite. There was a bridge and a hillside like this where I worked once in Nepal, and I can't help comparing the views. In Nepal, the terracing was of an almost erotic beauty, a perfect fusion of man and mountainside. It came from centuries of rubbing away at the hills until their most intimate contours were wholly known. In Ethiopia, the marriage of people and hillside seems arranged and awkward; how much of this work will endure?

*　　　　　*　　　　　*

We stay at the Ambessel Hotel – Dessie's best. When the man upstairs flushes his toilet, a sampling leaks out of the pipes onto your toilet seat – or into your lap, if you happen to be sitting there. When he takes a shower, the water pours through your ceiling. The restaurant menu features PIN APPLE BROKEN SLICE, though there isn't any this week. When the lights fail in the bar, pocket flashlights flick on all around, people who have stayed here before. The bill for five days is $42, and the place is just about worth it.

*　　　　　*　　　　　*

Here are the people I'm working with:

Mons Swartling, Swedish agriculturist and forester, WFP's man in Dessie. Mons grew up on the borders of Lapland and feels oppressed where the density of population is more than about one person per 10 square miles. (He feels oppressed in Dessie.) He has instructed Swedish Army recruits in winter survival techniques, worked with the Swedish Institute of Reindeer Management, and served with U.N. peacekeeping forces in Cyprus and the Middle East. With WFP in Uganda two years ago, he got into a quarrel with the Ugandan army. ("We want your food for our troops." "It's not for your troops, it's for the peasants, and you can't have it.") A week later, someone took a couple of shots at him with an automatic rifle. He nearly died and finally lost an arm – he wears a hook now instead. He has invented a table knife that screws into the prosthesis so he can slice his food. I say to him, "You should patent that; it could be worth a lot of money." He turns on me angrily: "Do you think I would try to make money from people that way?" Mons is a joy to work with.

Yeraswork Admassie, Ethiopian professor of sociology and our consultant for these three weeks. Yeraswork has seen foreigners blitz in and out of Ethiopia, seeking data to confirm their preconceptions, and he is not going to let us do that. Insistently, he makes us see the complexity of things, how difficult it is to generalize even about such apparent atrocities as forced villagization and resettlement. Yeraswork studied for seven years in Sweden (he and Mons speak Swedish with each other when they don't want the people at the next table to over-hear); among other things, he helped organize Ethiopian students all over Europe in opposition to the Emperor. In spite of that, when he returned to Ethiopia after the Revolution, he was tossed in jail. Now he works to insinuate socioeconomics into planning of rural projects, something he is doing for us with acute insight and great patience. The money he is earning may help get him to New York this summer to visit his wife and the eight-month-old son he has never seen.

Jane Brown, British forester with WFP in Addis. Jane got her degree from Cambridge and went straight off to Zambia to work on a World Bank industrial forestry project. She consulted for WFP after that and then took a staff job in China. Her illusions about development began to crumble there. The Chinese were superb at supplying information to their donors, information Jane increasingly saw to be misleading or outright invention. When she spotted damage spreading outward from projects, she was advised to keep silent. In Ethiopia now, she finds herself doubting the morality of working with an authoritarian government, the efficacy of food as a development resource, and her ability to make a professional impact on the projects she oversees. I share her concerns, and we spend a lot of time talking about how you digest insights like these, how you live them in your work.

What a grace it seems to work with people like this.

*   *   *

We are traveling again. Images: A baby donkey lies dead in the road, looking so very surprised and disappointed.

*   *   *

We meet with a group of farmers and local officials. We sit on a row of benches; they sit on the ground. We are in our bush-trav-el gear; they wear patched pants and shirts – the kind of things that come in bales from church groups overseas. I ask questions through an interpreter and then watch the long discussions that follow. Not understanding the language, I see only complex rhythms and tones of expression. Some people are bored now, some alert. Suddenly, the faces all set stonily in opposition to a line of questioning. A new thought, and the expressions shift, falling into dissonant clusters along lines of disagreement. It is like an orchestra that I am conducting through my questions. Do I really have a good enough ear to be playing this role?

In every such discussion with farmers, there emerge three lines of thought: the negative and discouraged view (with its implicit appeal for help), the "correct" line (tuned carefully to what the visitors want to hear), and the unexpected act of insight. In the last category, I think of the man who told us how use of the local hillsides has been changing. Before the 1974 Revolution, he explained, only the 10 or 15 most powerful people could take grass and wood from the hillsides, so the foliage was constantly renewed. After the Revolution, everyone used the hillsides, which were then stripped bare. Now, there is need for new ways of controlling access in order to increase biomass and distribute it fairly. So simple and direct. I wish we could make him Project Manager.

Simplicity is the exception. Every piece of information we have heard on this trip has, within 24 hours, been directly contradicted by some other piece of information. Work plans for each area are developed through consultation with local peasants; work plans are arbitrarily handed down by bureaucrats in Addis Ababa. Hillside closures sharply reduce the farmers' access to fodder; closures sharply increase access to fodder. Most of the trees live; most of the trees die. Farmers voluntarily maintain their soil bunds; farmers are so dependent on food aid that they maintain bunds only when paid.

It is the peril of leaving the office and confronting the real world. Back at headquarters, thoughts about development are clear, consistent, and abstract. Here in the field, the *facts* of development are often obscure and capricious, but are always very concrete. Between these modes of experience is a chasm so vast as to be almost unbridgeable. How can bureaucrat and peasant ever hope to touch?

ETHIOPIA

*　　　　　*　　　　　*

People used to make fun of the emperor for the high-flown poetry of his titles: King of Kings, Defender of the Faith, Conquering Lion of the Tribe of Judah. Now the poetry has been swept away by a revolutionary leader: Comrade Mengistu Haile-Mariam, General Secretary of the Central Committee of the Workers' Party of Ethiopia, Chairman of the Provisional Military Administrative Council, and Commander-in-Chief of the Revolutionary Armed Forces. Such crushing, dead weight in language like this.

It can be a hard place, this new People's Democratic Republic of Ethiopia. For example, practically anyone can throw you in jail: police, army, your neighborhood council. No conversation goes long without reference to this. "Just when we get our storekeepers trained, they get sent off to jail." "He was running the zonal office until he went to jail." "He's out of jail now and back on the job." Nobody seems to expect reasons. One person I met spent four years in prison for what his discharge papers called "suspicion of associating with a certain organization."

These are the lucky ones, since there have been periods when practically anyone might kill you. A woman I talk to is worrying about her daughter in the United States: "She is now my oldest child, since the government shot my son." Not many people here are without stories like these.

A government official: "To be in politics here, you have to be prepared always to lie, and to kill or be killed. I decided I'm not ready for those things, so I stay out of politics now."

It leads to a sense of defeat, a corruption of spirit. Friends speak of their grownup sons, bachelors at what by olden standards is an unreasonable age: "Today's youth don't like to marry; they like to spend their money to entertain themselves, drinking and smoking and going with women." In Addis Ababa, people talk ironically about the pursuit of the "3 Vs" – videos, Volvos, and villas. It is a game played with indecent success by Party members, government officials, merchants, whoever has access to the pie. Whatever the sins of the *ancien régime*, it is difficult to muster much affection for the "revolutionaries" who have followed.

*　　　　　*　　　　　*

Rule of Thumb (as expressed by a government official): "When you're using food as a payment to get work done, the most cooperative peasant is a hungry peasant." So we thrive on famine, and lose momentum when the harvest is good. Isn't there something wrong here?

The food is the carrot; there are also many sticks. We speak to a forester, who tells us how he shifts families and villages around to make room for his fuelwood plantations. (You there, move off this hillside; you there, move out of the area.) When he goes for a stroll among his trees, he takes bodyguards along to avoid embarrassment. We have heard similar stories from the folks at Soil Conservation who close off grazing lands to let them regenerate. (You there, move your animals off this hillside; you there, move yours out of the area.) In one respect at least, the Ethiopian Revolution has been a democratizing force: there are now many more people than before with the power to push other people around.

Still, working here forces you to think in new ways about coercion. For example, a group of villagers is told by the government to keep its animals off traditional grazing areas on nearby hillsides. In a year or two, the foliage has grown back and the hillsides stop washing into the valley. Slopes once bare are covered with grasses that can be cut and carried to the livestock.

"This is very good," says the leader of the local Peasants' Association. "But it works only because the Ministry of Agriculture tells us what to do. If the hillsides were given to us to control, the animals would be back the next day and the ground would be bare in a week."

The sense of helplessness and dependency has deep roots in Ethiopian social history. (Party and government have simply assumed the coercive role of the pre-revolutionary landlord.) In the absence of village solidarity and initiative, what is the correct role for the government to play? It is nasty to force people to close their hillsides; it is nasty to leave the hillsides open and watch them wash away. I'm glad I'm not the one who has to decide what to do.

*   *   *

More and more, these projects seem to me a metaphor for how things are in socialist Ethiopia. You can draw conclusions in alternative ways, depending on who you are:

Pollyanna: Over ten years, the projects have treated vast areas of Ethiopia with conservation works or planted them in trees. Even if this has been (say) only two-thirds effective, many thousands of people have benefited. Everywhere you go in the project areas, people tell stories of eroding hillsides that have been stabilized, once-dry springs that now flow again, improved soil fertility, reduced flooding, double- or triple-cropping on newly-irrigated land. In the course of all this work, fundamental issues are being confronted: how to manage woodlots for sustained yield of the products people most need, how to control access to communal resources. It is a vital learning process for both farmers and government officials. Little by little, new conservation practices are becoming ingrained in local culture, and land is being reborn.

Cassandra: Over ten years, these projects have treated less than 3% of the land originally defined as "highly eroded." Much of this work (say, one-third) has failed to last, and the benefits of the rest are often exaggerated. In addition, new areas are constantly becoming "highly eroded." At best, therefore, we are standing still. Even these results depend on a great deal of coercion, leaving farmers poised between gratitude for progress made and resentment at being pushed around. And the hard work is yet to come: most of the roadside areas (where food payments can easily be made) have now been treated, leaving much less accessible areas (which often have the most severe erosion) for the projects' next phases. Increasingly, the projects may consist of scattered pockets of social stress (where conservation works are underway) surrounded by great areas where degradation of the land proceeds unchecked.

Cassandra is probably telling the more accurate story, but there is at least some truth in both perspectives. Together, they reflect Ethiopia's troubled state: some people are better off; some people are worse off; many people are unaffected; the situation is deteriorating. What do you do with information like this?

We are driving back to Addis Ababa. Images: Rounding a curve, we burst upon a herd boy and his flock of sheep. In an instant, he has scooped the smallest lamb into his arms and leaped for the roadside. It is an act of instinctive love: I know my sheep, and my sheep know me. Let me finally remember that of Ethiopia.

Chapter 7
INDIA
1988[5]

The heat is infernal. In Delhi, everyone is delighted that temperatures have fallen to the low 100s – it has been much worse in recent weeks. Along breathless country roads, the sight of a buffalo lying contemplatively in a mud hole is enough to make you weep for a cold shower.

India is simply *too much*: too hot, too vast, too complex. There are 800,000,000 people here[6], 14 main languages and perhaps 200 dialects, desert and rain forest and Himalayan peaks, every possible religion. Nothing is quite the same as it is wherever you came from: the weather, the food, ways of eating, forms of greeting, music, roofing materials, cooking fuels, the alphabet, bargaining in shops, bureaucratic structures, smells, wildlife, land tenure systems, tree species, numbers (can you count in lakh and crore?), sports, religious taboos and imperatives, means of transport, gurus... If you appreciate overload, India is the place for you.

*   *   *

It is the forty-fourth anniversary of the death of Shri Vijaya Shanti, a Hindu holy man with followers throughout India. In the great courtyard of the temple must be a thousand people, men on one side

---

[5] Published in edited form (under the pen name "Douglas Stevens") as "The Forest and the Trees," in *Commonweal*, October 7, 1988.
[6] 1,325,000,000 in 2016.

of the central aisle, women on the other. On a massive stage, dozens of musical groups take turns singing praise of their guru. In a semicircle behind them are ranged the officers of the temple, prominent people of the city – and me.

I stumbled into this by following a parade through town: elephants, hand-drawn carts bearing musicians in full song, cows draped in bright cloth and flowers, their horns painted blue. Along the way, I talked with a group of young men selling souvenirs of the day. I asked for a poster, the guru beneath a tree on the shores of a lake, around him in perfect peace an audience of tigers, deer, peacocks, monkeys. "You must not misuse this poster," they warned me. "He is our god." Then they invited me here to the temple as their honored guest.

Dislocations. The music could be from India in any era, drums and harmoniums and crystalline voices. At the edge of the stage, though, is a Sinclair computer programmed by one of my newfound friends to flash messages through the evening: "JAI GURU DEV" (hail our guru and saint), "SHRI VIJAYA SHANTI," then the town from which comes the current group of singers, and once more "JAI GURU DEV," over and over. It is almost as hypnotic as the music.

The same party is happening everywhere. For days after this, as we drive across India, we pass cows now stripped of their garlands and drapery, their horns a steadily fading shade of blue.

*   *   *

The tiger lies down with the deer; the cow coexists with the computer. It is a day to savor, since much of India is not like this at all. Instead, every day, terrorists kill police somewhere, police kill terrorists, police beat demonstrators or shoot them, activists blow people up. In the home, women are burned alive for not providing their husbands with sufficient dowry. (In Delhi alone, there is a "dowry death" every 12 hours.) In the countryside, foresters battle with villagers...

Since I am in India to look at reforestation projects, I have a special interest in how foresters and villagers relate. These groups have a long, unhappy history of conflict. In 1945, Gopinath Mohanty wrote *Paraja*, a tale of tribal life that has become a classic. At the beginning of

Mohanty's novel, the Paraja tribesmen are living in a state of harmony with each other and their environment. This equilibrium is destroyed through the agency of the local forest guard, who tries to seduce a young village girl. Rebuffed, the guard brings a false case against the girl's father for cutting trees from the forest. The father and his sons are forced into bondage to a moneylender as the only means of paying the fine. By the end of the novel, the family has been destroyed and the life of the tribe badly shaken.

Such things really did happen – and are happening today. While I was in India, foresters clashed with villagers in a tribal area in the center of the country. According to press reports, the incident began after tribesmen tried to free a young man who had been beaten and detained by forest guards. The foresters lashed back at nearby villages, gang-raping one woman, beating people, arresting bystanders on a variety of false charges. The violence here was more direct and extreme than in the fictional *Paraja*, but it reflected the same, longstanding sense of strain between people and foresters.

In part, this stems from simple racism. As in *Paraja*, many forest villagers are from tribal groups. Some of the tribes were here long before the dominant Caucasians began to arrive from Central Asia, roughly 8,000 years ago. As India's "Indians," people from tribal groups are viewed with varying degrees of contempt. In conversation, they are known simply as "the tribals," as in "Look, ma, there's a tribal!" The foresters share this language, and the villagers know it.

*   *   *

We drive all afternoon to reach a remote plantation. For a time, I follow the tour prepared for us. Then I shed my escort and head into the forest, walking among the teak trees. For a long, peaceful moment there is silence, and then the most magical sounds begin. Blowing among the trees are little percussions of air, like wind chimes or drops of water falling into a pool. Drawn to the sounds, I find myself out of the forest and back at roadside. There, the mystery is explained: passing down the road is a herd of cows, their bells thunking dully as they head for home.

Not everyone finds romance in the cows. I am traveling with a British forester who quickly decides that cows cause degraded forests. "They're like locusts," he says, "sweeping through the forest in search of food." Reminded that Hindus consider cows sacred, he waves his arms. "We have to cast away all this juju," he says. "Bloody cows, they should all be killed and eaten." The Indians we're with grow quite silent when he gets like this.

Still, he has a point. For decades, the forests have been under great pressure from foraging livestock, as well as from commercial timber interests and land-hungry peasants. Although statistics on deforestation are shaky, even the range of possibilities is scary: since 1952, the area covered by forests has contracted by 20-40%, depending on whose estimates you believe. Perhaps 100 million acres of the remaining forest could be classified as "degraded," and 3.7 million acres of forest disappear entirely each year.

Bad things happen as a result. Firewood and building materials become painfully scarce. Soils lose texture and fertility in the absence of the root systems and leafy humus that trees used to supply. The problem is compounded as people collect dung to use as fuel instead of spreading this on their fields for manure. As deforestation spreads, rainfall becomes erratic. When the rains do fall, they wash quickly off the dead, compacted soils.

The foresters' instinctive response is to tighten control over the trees. Trenches are dug to keep livestock out of the forest; guards are posted to send people away. Scrubby trees are pruned back, and seedlings are planted to fill up empty spaces. Given time and a little help, the forest creates itself anew.

Any sense of satisfaction ends at the trench line, however. Outside the perimeter, people know only that they are being kept from things they desperately need. Everyone can think of better ways to use the forest: grazing hungry animals there, cutting trees for firewood and building poles. Most poignant are the landless (half the families in many forest villages), who are shut out from land they could use to grow food. When you have nothing to eat, or no fuel for cooking, "conservation" is an ugly and threatening word.

The threat is made all too visible. At each site we visit, the forest guards are drawn up on display. They are dressed in military khaki, a cascade of braid and stars and epaulets on their shoulders. Each wears a military beret (save the Sikhs, turbaned above the khaki). As we alight from our Land Cruisers, the guards greet us with a stamp of the foot and a crisp salute. The image they project is meant to intimidate, not to reassure.

*   *   *

The tension over the forests is resolved in standard ways. For example, foresters can accept money to look away as people cut trees. (Persistent rumor has it that to *become* a forester requires a bribe equal to a year's salary, money that is quickly recovered.) Alternatively, foresters who refuse to look away can simply be eliminated. (Rumor also has it that a couple of hundred foresters are murdered each year by villagers in need of wood.)

Increasingly, local people also use the political system to support their incursions into the forest. Especially at election time, you can always find a politician to stand behind you as you cut the forest department's trees and settle on its land.

This makes the foresters crazy and bitter. Almost universally, they have come to consider "democracy" a dirty word, a cloak for spineless vote-mongering at the permanent expense of the environment. The ex-colonial British forester I'm traveling with understands their frustrations: "If these tribals had cut the trees in the old days," he reflects nostalgically, "we'd just have knocked their heads together, eh?" But you are not supposed to do that now, and the foresters – and the forests – are suffering.

The foresters fight back as best they can. When possible, they have areas reclassified from "protected forests" (where villagers have some traditional rights) to "reserve forests" (where villagers have no rights at all). And they try to restore degraded areas, as in the projects we have been seeing. But more and more, it seems to them a losing battle.

Would things work better if heads could be knocked together? Possibly, if the foresters could see clearly into the heads they were knocking. Mere coercion cannot keep hundreds of millions of people out of the forest. Empathy is called for, in order to set a course for forest management that people can respect.

But empathy is not the foresters' most conspicuous quality. We are visiting a village where the forest department is assisting a national scheme for "tribal development." As the villagers cluster around to watch, we are told (by the foresters) about what has been provided during the past several years: a well for drinking water, an irrigation system, firewood and fodder plantations on village land, a community center. Once the foresters are finished, the head of the village council is brought on to testify to the revolution in living standards that these things represent.

As the speeches continue, I wander off down the road with a couple of villagers, members of the local tribe. They tell a different story. They've heard nothing about an irrigation scheme, nothing about firewood and fodder. Yes, there is a community center, but the head of the council keeps the key, and only his friends are allowed to use the place. As for the well, this was placed in a part of the village where the higher castes are concentrated. My tribal informants don't feel welcome there, so they go to the river for their water, as they've always done.

At this point, one of the foresters catches up with us. From now on, when I ask the villagers a question, the forester answers for them. Little by little, the scheme starts making sense again. The villagers drift away, but not in peace. There is little empathy at work here. Indian foresters may suffer from lack of control over people, but it is hard to have confidence in what they would do if "democracy" were curtailed and they were granted more power.

*   *   *

What can come of a situation like this? In one Indian state, $100 million is about to be spent on degraded forests. Over five years, this massive program will rehabilitate just 3.5% of the forest land now classified as "degraded." At such a pace, it would take 143 years to re-habilitate today's degraded areas. But new areas are degrading all the time, at least as fast as this program would rehabilitate old ones. The *best* that could happen is that things might remain in their present, disastrous state.

But the best cannot happen. Even now, desperate people everywhere bypass the guards and chip away at the forest. The pressure will grow with the population. At present growth rates, population in these areas would expand forty-fold over 143 years. It cannot really come to that, but there will inevitably be a great increase in the numbers of people and animals in need of the forest. *Whatever* the foresters do, the forests will be pushed back, the environment will deteriorate, and people will suffer.

*   *   *

I am talking with a group of farmers about their use of forest produce. Across the dirty track that bisects the village, a two-wheeled bullock cart is tipped forward on its poles, its bed in the air. A couple of curious children climb into the cart to watch us talk. Another child joins them, then two more. There is a child too many now, and the cart loses balance; it tips abruptly back onto its bed, children spilling into the dirt. If you were the type to worry, you could find a metaphor here for India itself.

After what I have seen this month, I worry.

TRAVELS WITH DAVID

Chapter 8

VIETNAM

MAY-JUNE 1991

Driving from the airport into Hanoi, we arrive at an area of small shops, like one of the poorer Indian areas of Nairobi – only denser, and stretching for miles along the roadside. Each shop specializes: along one short stretch of road, I see separate shops selling bicycle tires, fan blades, sandals, guitars, bicycle seats, soccer balls, caps, mirrors, plastic jugs, spools of wire...

Driving is near impossible for the thickets of bicycles and the unending lines of cars. "Things are quieter here in the countryside," says the driver. *Here in the countryside?* What should we expect of downtown Hanoi?

*   *   *

I am in Vietnam with a Dutch engineer to look at a project to rehabilitate sea dikes. Vietnam has 1,500 miles of these dikes, which protect perhaps 1,250,000 acres of land. In the best of times, the dikes are too low and too narrow, allowing seawater to seep through or spill over onto the cropland on the other side. In the worst of times, when the typhoons come, the dikes wash away and vast areas are inundated by the sea.

Every year, 8 to 10 typhoons hit Vietnam's coast. Every second year, one of these is a super typhoon, with winds of 100 mph or more. The damage these storms can do in a couple of days is enormous.

The effects are felt even when the storms stay away. Since high-yielding rice varieties are especially vulnerable to salty water, nobody will plant these where a typhoon might break the dike. Instead, people rely on local varieties (low-yielding but salinity-resistant). As a result, rice yields in the area are low even in "normal" years.

Our project is intended to do something about this. Given our food in exchange for their work, people in each area will raise their dike's level and broaden its base, compact the soil, turf the top, interlock rocks on the sides (called "rip-rap"), and plant a corridor of protective mangroves a few yards out to sea. Nobody is quite sure, but we think this could cut by more than half the number of years in which dikes are breached. I like the idea of trying.

*   *   *

The driver was right about yesterday's "countryside" being quieter than the city. The streets teem with bicyclists and the occasional "moto" (scooter). Still, there is something special about the traffic here. The collective movement is like a stream, flowing around the odd obstruction, building up behind barriers and then breaking through again to follow its course, ripples and swirls of bicycles dividing and coming together again.

Into the midst of this are dropped great noisy blockish things – cars – moving across the flow, separating the current, constantly blowing their horns, insisting on their autonomous, controlling presence. And yet, the flow of bicycles remains the core reality, the cars an obtrusion. I have often felt that the fastest insights into a culture come from watching its traffic, and I would bet that the pre-automotive spirit on these streets says much about inner life in the north of Vietnam. (I would also bet it is not like this in the south, but I won't get there on this trip to see.)

*   *   *

At 4:00 a.m., the pig starts to scream. There are conflicting theories as to what is being done to him: someone says his throat is cut first and then he is dumped into boiling water; someone else says he is simply popped straightaway in the pot and boiled to death. In either case, the screaming goes on and on. We say later in the car how hard it was to sleep through this. The man from the Ministry of Water Resources laughs – the people in the neighborhood, he says, cannot sleep if they do not hear the crying of the pig.

By 5:30, the children are gathering outside the school across the road to do calisthenics, and by 6:00 there are two games of soccer underway in mid-street, play flowing smoothly (if noisily, given the incessant blowing of horns) around the early morning traffic.

*   *   *

On the way to Thanh Hoa, we drive for hours past people transplanting rice into their paddy fields. I reflect (as I have often done in other countries) on what it must mean to be a "subsistence farmer." Every day, you work to grow food to eat; every day, you eat food you have grown. It must affect the spirit in so many ways unimaginable to me – I feel I am on one edge of a great chasm, they on the other.

The distance may perforce be narrowing – through their movement, not mine. As more and more people are born into the same space, land holdings grow smaller. Average farm size in our project area is now about half an acre. Even if you could double-crop the land (not everybody can), you would grow no more than 1,000 pounds of rice each year. This is one-half what you need to feed a family of five. To get money for the rest, you do other things too: salt-making, fishing, handicrafts, walking all day to the hills to collect firewood for sale in the market (a 65-pound bag of wood gathered, carried, and sold in this way will earn you up to 35 cents).

At some point in a process like this, you stop being a "subsistence farmer" and start being the "rural poor." Some move to cities and become the "urban poor," and a few of those become "upwardly mobile" – more and more like people I know. It all seems inevitable, and perhaps exactly what should be. Still, a part of me regrets the loss of that chasm as people stop living on the other side.

TRAVELS WITH DAVID

*   *   *

We are in the province where Ho Chi Minh was born, and the vice-chairman of the Provincial People's Committee seems pleased when I refer to Uncle Ho as one of the century's great leaders. As the conversation proceeds, I take a cautious step: "Was this area affected by the bombing during the war?" The vice-chairman says, "I don't remember"; and there is a long silence before we start talking again about typhoons and dike repair. Is the war (the "American War" here) off-bounds for discussion?

*   *   *

One of our big surprises: "sea dikes" here are seldom on the sea. I guess we had come with a vision of driving the Vietnamese coast, dipping occasionally into the water to cool off, standing on dikes and looking out to sea. The coast is protected by sand dunes, though, and the dikes are elsewhere, following the estuaries inland to where the "coastal" road travels south toward Ho Chi Minh City.

It leads us to an unanticipated, richer kind of travel. Site visits involve climbing onto the deck of a motorized junk and following the shore of an estuary seaward, inspecting dikes as we go. On our way, we pass through acres of fishnets, arcing gracefully above the water in anticipation of high tide. Small girls glide by in overgrown canoes, leaning back and working the oars with their feet, sole seemingly stuck to oar handle. In villages of fishing boats all clustered together, people come to their decks to see these strangers pass by.

Spotting an ornate stone arch near the mouth of one estuary, I ask if we can go look. Through the arch and among the trees is an ancient pagoda, a mix of Buddhism and Confucianism, the inner chamber sheltering a statue of the general who 500 years ago won a battle there against armies from China. An almost equally ancient caretaker opens the pagoda, lights joss sticks, shows us around. The place is nowhere near anywhere, approached from waters only fishermen pass over, and I wonder if he has ever had a group of visitors quite like ours before.

VIETNAM

*   *   *

Somewhere in Nghe Tinh province, I no longer know just where, in a government rest house. It was 101 degrees today, and we spent most of it outside, walking dikes and talking revetments. It is late evening now, but probably just as hot still in my airless room. I write by flashlight because the voltage is fluctuating wildly between perhaps 10% and 40% of normal, not enough to draw serious light from the single 15-watt bulb hanging from the ceiling. In the bathroom there is no light at all, nor is there toilet seat, toilet paper, soap, or any way of bathing save a bucket I had the foresight to fill this afternoon while the water was temporarily running. They have been trying to tell me all day that Nghe Tinh is a very poor province, especially in need of help, and this place drives home the point wondrous well. Perhaps we could have a food-for-work project to rehabilitate the government rest houses?

*   *   *

In Quang Ninh, the provincial vice-chairman said that 15 years ago, it would have been very dangerous for an American to drive around his province. Now, there would be no problem. That was as close as he wanted to get to talking about the war. So far, the only extended reaction I have gotten to my cautious questioning is a recurring, earnest plea for normalization of relations between Vietnam and the United States, along with a lifting of the American embargo. America's continuing attempts to isolate Vietnam are a major barrier to the country's development, and everyone seems to hope I can somehow convince my government to live finally in peace with them.

*   *   *

Mrs. Hoa interprets for us. She is a stick surmounted by great black eyes and awesomely high cheekbones, completely beautiful. Away from the meetings, we carry on conversations about small things, in simple English. I have had a good deal of experience talking English with basically non-English speakers, and I thought I knew most of the tricks, but Mrs. Hoa is a challenge.

In the meetings, things quickly get more complex. As mediated by Mrs. Hoa, we have exchanges like this: Q. How many cubic yards of earth are used each year to repair the dikes? A. If funds are available, the province can mobilize one million workers. Q. What kinds of improvements do you need for your pumping stations? A. In poor areas, when the typhoons come they knock down many people's houses. I'm glad I meditate a lot these days.

*   *   *

On to Quang Binh. In addition to riding in the Land Cruiser, standing on sea dikes, and sleeping, we eat and drink. Even in our meeting rooms (too grand a term? – sometimes a shed in some remote village), even there we are provided Coke, mineral water, bananas, cigarettes, beer, grapes, peanuts, tea, coconuts. Meals are more elaborate, sometimes seafood (steamed crabs, giant prawns, boiled and fried fish, clam soup – and this was just one meal), sometimes your basic Vietnamese sampler (chicken, shrimp, squid, rolled fried somethings, bean sprouts, spicy ground beef wrapped in some sort of fragrant leaf, chunks of grilled fish, soup, bread, rice...). This happens twice every day, lunch and dinner. Perhaps *we* should be asking *them* for food aid...

*   *   *

In Malawi, at the end of a day of driving between tall rows of maize, I would fall asleep in a liquid inner place all green, as if I were swimming under water. Here, falling asleep, vision opens to more concrete images from the day: masts of boats rocking gently at riverside; conical hat over white blouse over black trousers; a stretch of rice paddy ending at a river dike; thousands of people (each absolutely individual and distinct) weaving their bicycles around each other and by our Land Cruiser; roadside stretches of a hundred rice and noodle bars, each with its table outside of beer and mineral water bottles; many figures crouched around a map, a government photographer behind recording it all on film. In many cases, these are images I had hardly registered in the course of the day. Now they emerge, one by one, crystal clear, and say, "Look, look again."

*　　　　　*　　　　　*

An easy day, in our terms: six hours of separate meetings with officials of two provinces (issues both delicate and complex, the interpreter leading us periodically on long and perilous detours, me as mission leader either stage center or on very careful watch), plus nearly three hours of official banquets, lunch and dinner (vast quantities of food and drink, exchanges of toasts, speeches of welcome, thanks, goodbye).

As least we could sandwich in a late-afternoon hour at the beach, miles of brilliant white sand, waves just big enough to dive under, perfect bliss. As we were arriving, a young Vietnamese man trotted into the water to retrieve his wife, who was drifting slowly out to sea on a pink rubber ring. Trotting back, he swooped up his daughter and whirled her around, as she laughed and laughed. Then they got into an argument as to which way to go next, and the girl stood there pouting, an inflated plastic swan tucked under one arm. Then they were gone.

*　　　　　*　　　　　*

The vice-chairman of the Quang Binh Provincial People's Committee outlines the problems of his area, notably the difficult job of rebuilding after the war, planting more trees. He is the only person so far who has spontaneously alluded to the war, and during dinner I ask whether the tree planting was needed because of defoliation of the forests in this area. He immediately becomes impassive, and the conversation dies. I think the problem is that people simply don't know how to talk about these things with an American, and keep silent for fear of giving offense. Still, in the vice-chairman's remarks at our roundup meeting the war is there again, and the difficult job of rebuilding, like a pill stuck in his throat.

*   *   *

We crossed the 17th parallel this morning heading for Hue, and are now in what was once South Vietnam. We could tell we were approaching the dividing line by the number of abandoned bunkers along the road. Then an unremarkable bridge, and we were South. Of course, we all know it was once not so easy.

I have finally found someone anxious to talk about the war: Mr. Dan, the WFP "national officer" working on our project. (Rumor has it that he was an NVA infiltrator in the South during the war, but I think it is the kind of story you never quite verify.) At one point in the early '70s, Mr. Dan was at some sort of training center near the Ho Chi Minh trail, everyone in tunnels during the American bombings. Two of his classmates got curious one day, went up to see the fireworks, and got shredded, a couple of teachers as well.

The physical evidence builds up too. In Haiphong, we drove past the bombed-out shell of a cement factory. In Hanoi, the hospital that got the worst of the Christmas Bombing. Pilings of bridges that haven't crossed a river since the '60s. In Danang, an old woman clopping awkwardly past our hotel on a primitive artificial leg. At one point today, we drove past a church, cross still in place but the roof and a wall gone, the facade pockmarked by shell fire. I could only wonder who had tried to take shelter there; what had happened to them was obvious.

*   *   *

In the night, there is a thump in the room and then a series of anguished little cries, trailing off into silence. By the time I get my flashlight on, there is nothing to be seen. In the morning, a banana I had left on the table has been half eaten away. I think of the rats for which Vietnam's hotels are famous (I have seen only one, running across the floor of the bar at our hotel in Hanoi) and wonder what sort of show I have unwittingly been hosting here all night.

VIETNAM

*   *   *

An afternoon off to tour Hue. The Hue-UNESCO Working Group has a brochure on the city: "Tourists from all corners of the world have come to Hue to contemplate its beauty and enjoy its catchy songs." There is even an example of a catchy song:

> In the tranquil atmosphere, the Dieu De Temple bells
>   ring and drums resound
> Over the twelve-spanned Truong Tien bridge
> And reach Thanh Long palace on the left and Bach Ho
>   palace on the right
> The melodious tune of a peaceful life.

Though we hear no catchy songs, life is peaceful enough as we make our way around. At the Citadel, the heart of the old royal capital, Vietnamese tourists come and go, thinking who knows what of this old and complex symbol of Vietnamese nationalism, feudalism and (much of the present city having been built in the early years of French rule) European colonialism. I can't help noticing the scars of bullet and shell on the inside walls. Michael Herr's descriptions (in his book *Dispatches*) of the battles during the Tet holidays in 1968 float through my head, but that is history now.

Outside the walls, several miles up the river, is the seven-story Thien Mu pagoda. A monk opens the doors, and we stroll around taking pictures and being tourists. After the rest of the group wanders out, I sit cross-legged in front of the Buddha and let the breathing flow. Almost at once the group trails back in looking for me, breath turns to sigh, and out we all go.

Behind the pagoda are the monks' quarters. In a small garage is an ancient car on cement blocks. In the window of the car is an old photo of a monk who has set himself on fire and is seated in flames in a Hue street – *the* photo, one we all remember from those years. Behind the burning monk is parked a car, in which the monk had ridden to the place and from which gasoline had been siphoned for the immolation. The car here on blocks is *the* car, and this is the monk's pagoda. It is quite a while before I can take all this in.

I ask today's interpreter, supplied by the Hue Department of Water Resources, to find out if the monks here know Thich Nhat Hanh, the wartime activist monk whose recent book on meditation I have been reading. The interpreter is young and nervous and very politically correct, and this request to move outside the planned program obviously bothers him a lot. "They will not know him," he says, and walks away. In careful English, I ask a monk the same question. He smiles softly: "Yes, he was in Hue, now is in France. Everyone here loved him very much." The interpreter reappears, interrupts: "You are interested in Buddhism?" he asks. Not knowing what kind of minefield I am walking myself (and the monks) through, I say only "Yes" and off we go. The tour is over.

*   *   *

The highways are for the people here. We are on Route 1, the main road between Hanoi and Ho Chi Minh City. Mile after mile, we drive over a carpet of yellow-green – people have spread the paddy from the current harvest across the road, and we thresh it as we drive by. We weave among farmers raking away the rice straw, sweeping the rice into piles. Farther along, several children squat in the center of our lane, intent on some game they are playing with stones on the roadway. At another place, someone has marked off a square yard of Route 1 with stones and is drying chilies on the tarmac.

*   *   *

In Danang. The chairman of the People's Committee hosts us for dinner on this last night of our field trip. Seated next to me is Madame Minh, who was ambassador to Italy when the World Food Program first got involved with Vietnam 15 years ago. Madame Minh's grandfather was Phan Chau Trinh, a great revolutionary leader who was condemned to death by the French in 1907, reprieved, and instead deported to France, where he was one of Ho Chi Minh's teachers.

Madame Minh herself is something of a historical figure in Vietnam, among other things having served for several years in the 1970s as part of the negotiating team in Paris led by her cousin, Madame Binh. I ask Madame Minh what it was like to deal with Henry Kissinger. The sudden seriousness in her expression is mixed with something else I cannot quite define: incredulity? sadness? "He is a very intelligent man," she says, but with "*aucun sentiment humain*" – no human feeling. She is clearly as strong a personality as Henry, but she keeps going far beyond where he stops, and the pain she must have experienced in dealing with such a person is still on her face.

I tell her how moving – and how difficult – I find it as an American to be visiting Vietnam for the first time. She immediately reaches out to reassure me. "What is past is past," she says. "We look forward to a future in which our countries will live in friendship. But we distinguish between the people of America and the government of America. This is something that Chairman Ho Chi Minh taught us to do from the very beginning. I have many American friends, and I know people in America are working to convince the government to normalize relations with Vietnam. Even during the war, we knew that many people were opposing the government's policies, and this was extremely important in bringing the war to an end. We are not bitter about the GIs who came here – many of them were victims too, and many have come back to visit us, sometimes with their families." This comes out not as formula but as deep and simple sincerity, and all I can think to say to her is that it takes a large soul to say such things.

This conversation is in French, which Madame Minh renders into Vietnamese from time to time for the benefit of the People's Committee chairman and the others nearby. They seem greatly uncomfortable with such an unscheduled airing of delicate matters, but Madame Minh and I keep it up all through dinner.

Afterwards, she invites us to her home, which the family has turned into a private museum to her grandfather. Cabinets full of dusty old manuscripts, ancient photos, books about her grandfather or anthologies in which his poetry appears, in the middle of the room a Vietnamese-style altar behind which is a portrait of the man himself. Even during the *ancien régime* (the period of American-installed governments), nobody dared touch such a shrine. Here is the continuing center of Madame Minh's life, guarding the memory of her great ancestor. She is a formidable woman, and I leave shaken by the evening.

*   *   *

We are writing up the project now, and I like it a lot. The Vietnamese have long experience in standing up to assaults from land and air (the Chinese, the French, the Americans) as well as from sea (killer typhoons with names like Cecil and Jerome). They can handle it alone if need be, building deeper tunnels or taller dikes, but a bit of help from friends is always welcome. According to Madame Minh, all those antiwar noises twenty years ago made a difference; maybe a little food aid can make a difference now, helping to hold back the sea. It has been a long, long time since I have seen a development project that felt this right.

*   *   *

The final round-up meeting with senior government officials. Among other things, this calls for the kinds of formal exchanges at which I have become fairly adept in my time here. "On behalf of the mission, I would like to thank the Vice-Minister for his extremely helpful remarks. (Things we have heard a hundred times already.) His staff worked exceptionally hard to prepare for our mission and to meet our many requests for further information. (True, and we hope the compliment registers with the boss.) Although we fully support the project, we must recognize that the World Food Program is currently in a period of severe resource constraints. (You will get half of what you asked for, a message it is useful to have delivered by me rather than the head of our local office, who has to stay on and live with you.) Nonetheless, our belief in the project is such that we will argue vigorously in Rome for the greatest possible level of support. (Basically, we are all good guys here.) Thank you. (Thank you.)"

VIETNAM

*   *   *

All through, waiting for the Thai Airways flight to lift off from Bangkok for Rome. *Newsweek* in the magazine rack, the cover story "Hello Vietnam" (or "cashing in on Asia's last frontier"). In spite of the American embargo, says *Newsweek*, savvy investors – lured by a wealth of natural resources, abundant export commodities, and a disciplined work force hungry for jobs – are betting on Vietnam's future. Although offshore oil is still the biggest prize Vietnam has to offer, farsighted entrepreneurs in low-overhead export markets have already recovered their investments many times over. Once Washington decides to give the country a chance, Vietnam may finally be able to realize its enormous economic potential.

It is deeply disturbing: I do not recognize this place, I have never been there. *Newsweek's* Vietnam is unidimensional, unidirectional, chilling. We tried to bomb the suckers back to the Stone Age, now we will club them to death with wads of money (all those disciplined little people hungry for jobs), the stick and the carrot, *we will win yet.*

It is doubly dislocating because the Vietnam where I spent the last three weeks seemed so *familiar.* It could be jarringly so. Once, floating down an estuary towards the sea, our junk became a gunboat, the foliage along the bank suddenly a screen for snipers to lie behind. Edgy chatter all around: let's call in a little artillery, put a few rounds into that sonofabitch on his bicycle over there, waste a buffalo or two just to keep the gooks awake. Then Mrs. Hoa was back and Mr. Dan and the Dutch engineer, and we were talking about the amplitude of waves and the height of dikes above MSL. That felt familiar too.

And all those other images, already so well known: people transplanting their rice, swirls of bicycles, a slender figure in white blouse and dark trousers, chilies drying on Route 1. We have all lived Vietnam a thousand times, and here it was for the thousand-and-first, neither more real nor less than all the times before. I waited twenty years for this trip, twenty-five, and never realized how much of a homecoming it would turn out to be.

TRAVELS WITH DAVID

Chapter 9

SUDAN

SEPTEMBER-OCTOBER 1992

Tex-Mex night at the Khartoum Hilton coffee shop, limp enchiladas and refried beans barely warmed from the can. The affluent and the expatriate are here, washing down the ersatz food with Pepsis and karkadeh (a drink made from hibiscus flowers; no alcohol in the Islamic Republic). It is like a cocoon, all air-conditioned and Musaked. Is this really the Sudan you read about in the papers?

Well, yes, at least beyond the Hilton door. Rumors are that 300 civilians were murdered by the army this week in Juba, including Sudanese employees of the U.S. aid program (AID), the U.N. Development Program (UNDP), and the European Community (EEC). Juba is the capital of Sudan's southern region, whose (largely Christian) black inhabitants have been in revolt for years against the Arabs of the north. The central government has effectively been taken over by Muslim "fundamentalists," whose contempt for the "primitives" of the south is pretty scary. This is now a war without quarter.

The Juba massacre was the aftermath of attacks a month or two ago by the rebels, who reportedly walked into town one night, found the army asleep in its barracks, and shot the place up before being driven away again. Lacking anybody else to get even with, the army has been working on the local population. The magazine *SUDANOW* says, "The government forced the [rebel] Garang troops away from Juba, and made the area safe for every body." That seems about right.

Explaining the events, *New Horizon* says that "the [AID] person concerned was caught using a radio-set to direct rebels to bombard certain locations in Juba town. He confessed his crime before the court that tried him." You can bet on that. (*New Horizon* is the local English-language paper, and it has a style all its own. This week's banner headline, over a story of some anti-Sudanese skullduggery by the Saudis, reads "SAUDI VEIL UNMASKED.")

Nobody here really believes that any of the people killed in Juba were "directing rebels." Their mistake was to be working for Western relief agencies, which are being targeted by the army for their allegedly pro-rebel sympathies. *New Horizon* warns that other people "working for some organizations" may still "be penalized in accordance with applicable laws." If this goes on, the agencies that are feeding Juba may have to close down.

Juba is simply not a place to be. Supposedly, Afghan and Iranian mujahedin are serving there with the Sudanese. For companionship, they find the wives of men being held in prison and offer not to kill their husbands in return for sex. Or so the story goes. (There are so many stories...)

* * *

I am here as part of a mission to evaluate a $15 million drought-response project slapped together by UNDP when the rains failed in 1990. By no coincidence, the UNDP office in Khartoum had just discovered it had $15 million of unspent funds it was about to lose; and the drought gave it a perfect rationale for unloading the money in a hurry.

By December 1990, UNDP/New York had approved a "Special 1991 U.N. Drought Operation in the Sudan" (SUNDOS). SUNDOS was to use the $15 million for a bunch of worthy activities: borehole-drilling, support to state planning activities, food-for-work schemes like building reservoirs and schools or digging wells. The work itself was to be implemented by groups like UNICEF, CARE, Save the Children (U.K.), Sudanese Red Crescent, the International Labor Organization (ILO), and several government agencies. The World Food Program (WFP) was responsible for getting 9,000 tons of food to food-for-work sites in the northern parts of Kordofan and

Darfur, where the drought was most severe. Everything was supposed to get done before the next harvest (in December 1991), easing people through a rough year by providing work and water. My group is here to see what actually happened.

There are seven of us, three expatriates (me on behalf of WFP, a Danish consultant for ILO, and an American hired by UNDP as mission leader) and four Sudanese (representing UNICEF, CARE, and the Ministries of Labor and Finance). After a couple more days of meetings with agencies here in Khartoum, we'll be off to "the field" to see what traces SUNDOS has left.

*   *   *

Having made it through another dinner at the Hilton coffee shop (Italian night tonight: soggy pizza and tasteless pasta), I am wandering through the lobby when the elevator door opens and Yasser Arafat walks out. He is immediately surrounded by young men with automatic weapons and whisked out the door. He comes to town often, I'm told (he was flying from Khartoum when his plane went down in the desert last summer), a matter of managing his investments and keeping in touch with PLO groups based here. The U.S. claims that the hills of northern Sudan are full of "terrorist" training camps (who knows how much truth there is to this), one reason of several for the edgy relationship between Washington and Khartoum these days.

*   *   *

Our little Twin Otter taxis out between giant Aeroflot cargo planes, on charter to the U.N. for carrying relief supplies. We take off in a hundred yards of runway, bank over an airplane carcass that has been dragged off into the weeds, and begin to climb over Khartoum.

It seems a sandbox city, low earthen houses rising from little more than raw desert. Much of this is squatter housing, on land grown valuable as the city has spread around it. I've been told by someone in the Forest National Corporation that changes are in store: after twenty years in one of these houses, his assistant has just been given two weeks to move out. After that, the area will be bulldozed by the army and the land given to "certain people" with connections in high places. Anybody left in the area when the army moves in will be bused into the desert and left there.

The army is good at this by now. A million people, mostly southerners forced into Khartoum by the war, have been bused out of town and their shacks torn down in the last couple of years. A lot of people were killed in the process, and a lot more died in the deserts they were dumped into. Perhaps 500,000 remain in camps 20-30 miles from town, barely surviving on the food the relief agencies are allowed to truck in. To make their status absolutely clear, I'm told, southerners are forced to register with Arab names in order to get food; those who insist on retaining their identity are left to starve.

Gaining altitude, we cross the White Nile, more brown than white at the end of the rains. Our plane is a UNDP charter from AirServ ("non-profit humanitarian air transport"), and it just about holds our mission members, somewhat scrunched up. I sit in the front to watch the pilot and indulge my fantasies of flying the plane. (Walter Mitty with a laissez-passer.) Maybe this time I'll have my chance: the pilot flew 15 hours yesterday, and as we level off, his eyelids grow heavier, blink, close... and then slowly open again.

After the best rains since 1988, the desert's thousand shades of orange-brown are mottled with patches of green like fine woodland moss, grasses that were not there two months ago and that by Christmas will be gone again, their seed mixing invisibly with the sand to await the next rainy year.

*   *   *

In El Obeid, we have a 6:30 breakfast of tea and halvah and boiled eggs with pure white yolks and are on the road by 7:00. After days of talks in Khartoum and then here, Sudan finally opens up to us and we are off into Kordofan. Acacias and baobab trees grow among fields of millet and sorghum; gardens of sesame and hibiscus are scattered here and there. Camels and donkeys rest alongside the road, egrets circulating among them in search of bugs to eat. Men in djellabas and women in clothes all color and flowers watch us go by. Part of the time we are driving in grass so thick someone has to walk ahead of the car to look for ditches, part of the time we are slaloming across sands so broad our half-dozen Land Cruisers fan out and race each other across the dunes. We're sure not in Kansas any more.

For twenty minutes, far from El Obeid, we drive through a great herd of camels – a thousand, maybe more, newborns on spindly, uncertain legs scattered generously among them. In their midst is their owner, an old man in faded brown robes, resting all unhurried under a patched skin stretched across some poles. In the markets of Aswan, forty days trek from here, each of his camels would fetch as much as $800, which means that the old man under the patched skin is the better part of a millionaire – on paper (if he had paper). He is likely to know this perfectly well, and to find it perfectly irrelevant.

He is exceptional. The droughts of 1984-1985 and 1988 wiped out most of the region's livestock. Earlier, our mission leader found a one-time herder who lost everything over those years. So few animals remain in the herder's own area that his son runs away in fright now when he sees a cow. Not that they could probably manage animals anymore if they had them: the traditional southern end of their grazing range has been taken over by the government for mechanized farming schemes.

After seven hours on the road (or on the sand, there being no road), we arrive in Sodari. The commissioner is there to meet us, and we all crowd into a small, tin-roofed school built through a SUNDOS food-for-work scheme. The temperature inside is in the low millions, the air absolutely still, everyone seems to be giving speeches. On a corner of the table in front of me are a fly and a tiny ant, not much bigger than the fly's front leg. The fly edges up sideways to the ant, turns jerkily around to face it, advances. (Do flies eat ants?) At this, the ant stops wandering aimlessly around and charges the fly. (Do ants eat flies?) The fly backs away, they both bob and weave, retreat to neutral corners, preen a bit, then move in on each other again. (Do ants dance with flies?) I can't stay awake. The ant and the fly keep doing whatever they're doing, the meeting drones on... and on....

*　　　　　*　　　　　*

Not far south of here are the Nuba Mountains, where Leni Riefenstahl took the photos for her book *The Last of the Nuba*. Her title was more prescient than she realized: with ruthless efficiency, the government is busy turning the Nuba into corpses or slaves. Unnumbered thousands have been massacred, and tens of thousands more have been driven from their homes. Many of the survivors have been forced into what amounts to slave labor, some in the households of northern Arabs, some on the farms that ate up the grazing lands of the herder we met the other day.

*　　　　　*　　　　　*

I have been reading the project monitors' field trip notes, which I find constantly engaging. After a trip to four rural councils, Anwar Mohamed reports, "Tremendous rats' attack on the lands has caused deep concern in most of the area." I'd be deeply concerned too if I were being attacked by tremendous rats.

There is a candor in some of this material that would never appear in any report a head office would produce. In Al Hamadia village, according to Abdel Gadir Ahmed:

> The project has distributed the sum of 600 chicks for 60 farmers, 10 chicks per farmer, and the price will be deducted in installment. The idea appreciated and welcomed by the rural and some obtained good strain of poultry for dual purpose i.e. egg and meat. But unfortunately most of them attacked to death by new castle disease that cause a tremendous losses among farmer's poultry.

In other words, by distributing infected stock, the project killed off all the local chickens.

This isn't the only disturbing information we are picking up. SUNDOS gave UNICEF $1 million to dig 700 boreholes in North

Kordofan during 1991, which they did. It turns out, though, that UNICEF's own budget had already provided for digging 700 wells in *South* Kordofan. UNICEF just shifted their drilling rigs to North Kordofan from South Kordofan, where they dug 700 *fewer* wells than planned. In other words, 700 wells got relocated, but no extra drilling actually got done by UNICEF in Kordofan as a whole. What did UNICEF do with the $1 million? (We never will find out.) The aid business is full of little mysteries like this.

The still worse news is that other parts of the project never got started at all. SUNDOS was supposed to distribute 4,600 tons of food in 1991 through food-for-work (FFW) schemes in N. Kordofan; they actually used 215 tons (including the food exchanged for work on the school we visited). During the same period, 1,220 tons of food went for FFW activities that would have gone on even if SUNDOS never existed. What was the point?

*   *   *

The bells begin to ring as the sun is going down, and I abandon the guesthouse to follow dusty streets to what turns out to be the Catholic cathedral of El Obeid. By 6:00, perhaps 500 people are crowded inside, 90% men (the few women mostly by themselves down an aisle at one side), 95% Sudanese (a lot of them southerners forced north by the war). The chorus was rehearsing as we came in – a driving, Missa Luba sound – but everything is quiet now.

After a few minutes, a man steps to a microphone to make a brief announcement in Arabic. All I catch is the ending, "inshallah" (if Allah wills it), which takes me briefly aback until it registers that of course Allah is Allah, for Christian and Muslim and Jew. There are differences in detail among the faiths – which son Abraham intended to sacrifice (Isaac, whose own sons founded the Jewish nation, or Ishmael, who founded the Arab nation), the small matter of whether Jesus was prophet or son of God – but Allah is always the same.

We wait in silence, and I can study the great painting that covers the wall behind the altar: a vast desert landscape, all stark but for a few palms at one edge. At the center, rising straight from the sand, carpeted stairs climb to a massive throne. On the throne, draped in Renaissance blues and reds, is a distinctly Caucasian Mary holding a blond baby Jesus. A half-dozen Baldovinetti angels hover protectively on clouds overhead. Off to one side is an Arab in heavy robes, kneeling reverently in the sand. There is more than one message here.

We wait some more, and I begin to guess what the announcement earlier must have been: "The priest is coming soon, inshallah." At 6:45, late for an appointment back at the guesthouse, I give up. As I leave, the 500 sit silently, waiting for their priest.

*   *   *

The wali (state governor) of Kordofan has invited us to a farewell luncheon in the countryside. When we get to the security checkpoint at the edge of town, they won't let us through. The security man who has been keeping an eye on our group arrives to explain, and they won't let *him* through. We point out that we are guests of the wali, but they send us back into town. Who is in charge here?

Who is in charge anywhere in Sudan? There is a president, and these state walis, all of whom are beholden to the National Islamic Front, which is run by shadowy figures behind the scenes (perhaps from the Islamic Brotherhood, whatever that really is), supported (or is it controlled?) by one or more overlapping (or is it competing?) security services. Getting stuck on the way to the wali's picnic is small beer (sorry, small karkadeh) compared with what *can* happen to you in a system like this.

*   *   *

We are back on the UNDP plane, headed from El Obeid to El Fasher, a big hop farther into nowhere. El Fasher is 300 miles from the nearest paved road, closer to Chad and Libya than to Khartoum. To ship food from Port Sudan to El Fasher costs WFP three times as much as getting it from Canada to Port Sudan, a lot of the difference being the premium paid for getting things trucked hundreds of miles along sand tracks through armed bandit country.

SUDAN

Once airborne, the pilot cranks up his computerized navigational system and enters "El Fasher." Based on what I saw on the way to El Obeid, the thing should display our recommended compass heading and other flight details. This time, though, the screen flickers and then reports: "No program available; use dead reckoning." It feels a little like diving off the edge of the world.

*　　　　*　　　　*

Riding into town, we hear the week's local news. Some of El Fasher's luminaries were caught drinking home brew in the house of a local pharmacist, and the wali for Darfur State himself came by to smell their breaths and pronounce them in violation of shariah law. The wali is a fundamentalist's fundamentalist, and he had them publicly lashed. As host of the party, the pharmacist was also sentenced to seven years in prison and fined $4,000. There is a demonstration in town today, thousands of people gathering to praise the wali and urge him to hang tough.

At the Government guesthouse, the ILO member of our team and I check out the room we are going to be sharing. Electric switches – wires exposed – hang from walls stained the yellow-brown of the sand outside. Wavering insecurely over our heads, a ceiling fan vaguely circulates hot air, particles of dust settling onto the tattered covers of our sagging beds, drifting across the unmatched lengths of dirty-green carpeting. Along one wall is a great wooden wardrobe, all its doors locked and no key in sight. That compensates for the door of the room itself, which neither locks nor latches – we have to wedge it shut with a piece of cardboard to keep it from banging in the breeze. There is no light in the bathroom, or toilet seat, or functioning shower, and the grime on the tub is built up in layers that could only appeal to an archeologist. All in all, it is a lot better than the places where we stayed in El Obeid.

In fact, the place has its own kind of charm. One of the bathroom windows is shuttered, and a pair of small birds are building a nest between shutter and the window glass inside. We eye each other through the glass as I ladle water from a bucket for a sort of shower, then they flicker out through the slats in search of nest materials.

Outside the other bathroom window, a woman sweeps a sand path with a broom of crudely bound straw. What seem to be a dozen puppies tumble around their whippet-thin mother as the local variety of pigeons, their great saucer-eyes blood red, coo overhead. Just beyond is a brilliant bougainvillea, and then a broad wedge of sand flecked this week with sparse grass. A man crosses on a donkey, his wife walking behind. Goats lie in the shade of trees.

At the bottom of the slope is a pond swollen by the last of the rains, absurd here in the desert, cars driven axle-deep into the water for washing, boys splashing alongside. Past the pond, sand-colored buildings rise gently upward toward the mosque. In the distance is a low range of hills. For a long moment as I stand looking at this, the world seems perfectly at peace.

*   *   *

We are roughly north of the refugee camp of Meiram. There are perhaps 100,000 people there, trapped between the war to the south and a hostile government to the north. Waiting for our plane in Khartoum last week, I talked with a Sudanese relief worker on his way back to the camp. "The government is making sure that no word gets out," he said; "but even though food is arriving, it is desperate there. The children especially are weak, and the chill of the rains is too much for many of them. Every time the rains come at night, we spend the next morning burying children."

One thing the government does for the children – who come mostly from Christian families – is teach them the Koran. If you somehow get permission to visit the camp, those children who made it through the night will be lined up to recite Koranic verses for you.

Meiram is only one camp of many. WFP and the agencies we work with are feeding more than 3 million displaced Sudanese just now, a third of whom have been driven from their homes in the last year alone.

A lot of people don't make it to camps. Last year, annoyed at being harassed by rebels along the rail line to Wau, the army torched all the crops in the area. Some of the farmers ended up dead, some in places like Meiram, and some alongside the Nuba as slave labor on government farms. Which were the lucky ones?

*   *   *

I take a day off from SUNDOS to look at some food-for-work activities WFP has been supporting in the area: dune stabilization, shelterbelts, community forests. There is a lot of enthusiasm among the forestry extension workers; and in return for food rations, one group of 125 village women is planting trees communally for firewood. They have planted about an acre and a half so far, and will do more next year.

Still, it is painfully apparent that all the world's community forestry mistakes of the past fifteen years are being made again here. For example, although the women's trees are enough to meet the annual firewood needs of no more than five families, arrangements have yet to be made for the rationing of this precious resource. Leaving decisions like this until the trees grow up is an almost certain recipe for serious conflict, the appropriation of the trees by the most powerful person in the area, and the inevitable failure of the scheme. We talk about ways to deal with the problem, but I am reminded again of the truism that some of the worst damage in the development business is done by some of the best-intentioned people.

Driving back to town, we see watermelon leaves beginning to show above the sand. Watermelons in this part of Sudan are melons for water: by January, especially in the desert north and east of here, wadis and wells will dry up, leaving many people dependent on the water of the melons. Everyone gets a share, says the Sudanese man I am traveling with: the people drink the water, the goats and donkeys eat the rinds, and the seeds are dried and sold in markets as far away as Egypt. The idea of watermelons as something you have for dessert on picnics strikes him as very strange indeed.

*   *   *

One of our little group for yesterday's field trip was an over-wrought Indian forester on contract with the U.N., obviously struggling to survive here. For the most part, expatriates in places like these are a fairly desperate lot. Example: Chris, back in El Obeid, a little Australian with a vaguely defined background ("B.AppSc. [Rural Tech] Hons," says his card) who works on a U.N. project to restock the desert with gum arabic trees. Chris is divorced, and his ex-wife and daughter are with UNICEF in Phnom Penh. Every evening, he sits on the back porch of the Agricultural Research guesthouse looking through the screen, past a barrel of water, at a wall, the BBC World Service on the radio and a Pepsi in hand. For the occasional change of pace, there is the Syrian Club, a few wobbly card tables in the sand, where the couple of dozen expatriates in town congregate to drink their Pepsis. That is it for El Obeid.

Here in El Fasher, even closer to nowhere, there is still less. At dinner one night I meet Lennart, a Swedish regional planner with a hopeless regional planning unit (in a place like this, what's to plan?). Lennart spends his week waiting for *The Economist* to come so he can look for another job. We are dining at the house of Sakaria, a heavily bearded Gujarati engineer with the Special Public Works Program. Most of Sakaria's guests tonight are rather formal Sudanese, turbaned and djellaba-clad, but he presides with great potbelly protruding over colonial shorts, totally out of place.

"How's life?" someone asks Sakaria as we arrive. "No life without wife," he replies matter-of-factly (he has just put his family on the plane back toward Gujarat, and will see them next year sometime), and goes off to fix us our (non-alcoholic) drinks. The evening ends at 9:45, since Security has just ruled that all CD cars (that's us) have to be off El Fasher's roads by 10:00. Thus El Fasher: there is not even a Syrian Club here for variety.

This is only the beginning of the isolation. If you want to call home (Stockholm? Ahmedabad?), you have to radio someone in Khartoum who gets your family on the phone (inshallah) and then relays messages back and forth. If you are off the part of the power network that serves the hospital (and is therefore kept more or less functioning), you probably don't have electricity to run your radio and can't even do that. Mainly, you can sit and look at your wall. These are Graham

Greene characters in a country that forbids even the consolation of alcohol. They endure, I'm not quite sure how.

*   *   *

According to a field trip report from one of the project monitors here, "The situation in Goz Marakh is a bit queer. The work goes on zigzagly which depends on the availability of their Daf truck, which appears once and disappears four days." There is a lot of zigzagliness in this project, we are finding, and I'm glad the monitors are there to help point it out.

All in all, SUNDOS is not looking good. SUNDOS was designed to keep people alive and in place, largely by getting food into drought areas. What SUNDOS actually *did*, however, is hardly noticeable. Taking N. Kordofan and N. Darfur together, most of the action during 1991 consisted of getting relief food into the area (nothing to do with SUNDOS), 97,450 tons of it. SUNDOS added 265 tons of food to this, at a cost of $15 million.

Something went badly wrong here, and it is not hard to see what it was. The SUNDOS approach depended on "rapidly operationalizing" a wide range of activities that take time to get started. At best, food-for-work projects in places like these require so much planning and supervisory skill that their scale must be modest. Given the quantities of food needed in the area during the 1991 emergency, SUNDOS could never have been expected to have a discernible impact. As a development agency, UNDP should have known this; but their panic to spend $15 million overrode whatever sense they might otherwise have had. Nobody connected with the exercise is looking good at this point.

*   *   *

We are sitting in the security office, which is a tin-roofed, mud-walled hut in the sand at the edge of town. In order to leave for Khartoum tomorrow we have to register, a process that involves forms, fingerprints, passport photos, official stamps of various sorts, and a lot of time. We also have to get permits to take our cameras and radios with us, so those things need to be examined. All this to travel from one Sudanese city to another. The hut has automatic rifles stacked in one corner, and we briefly consider seizing them and running amok. It is too hot for that, though, so we sit and sit instead. Will we ever get out of here?

*   *   *

We made it: back in the Khartoum Hilton, with Tex-Mex night to look forward to again. Floating in the pool, dead tired, I watch a fingernail paring of a moon hanging in the palest of evening blue skies, wisps of cloud drifting by. When we left Malawi in 1984, the office accountant, Mr. Mkoola (drunk as always and morose at our leaving), said: "Wherever you are, you can look at the moon there, and I'll look at the moon here, and we'll be looking at the moon together." As I have done in a number of strange places since, I find myself wondering if Mr. Mkoola is looking at the moon tonight.

*   *   *

A couple of U.N. people and a journalist were killed in the South this past week, swept up in quarrels between two rebel factions. The WFP people in the area had left the day before for a meeting in Nairobi. One of those killed got caught in a crossfire. The other two were wounded and taken off by one of the rebel groups, which apparently treated their injuries, held them for three days, and then shot them. There are no good guys in this war.

*   *   *

One of the Sudanese members of our mission is late for this morning's meeting. A bunch of people at Khartoum's Industrial Research Institute have just been fired, no reasons given (the fundamentalist thought police need never explain themselves), and one of the ex-researchers has been at our team member's house trying to figure out where to go next.

The IRI people are not alone. Another of our team is leaving the country at the end of the week, having himself been fired a couple of months ago from his job as a professor of sociology at the University of Khartoum. In line with the university's new policy of Islamicization, he was instructed to start teaching Islamic Sociology this year, in Arabic instead of English. When some of the professors in various faculties questioned the pace at which this was all happening (there were no teaching materials on hand in Arabic, and what *are* "Islamic Sociology" and "Islamic Mathematics" anyway?), twenty of them were sacked.

They are perhaps not so unlucky. Fundamentalist vigilantes among the students have reportedly been murdering other students on campus this year.

What do acts like these have to do with Islam? I suspect not much. "Fundamentalism" is actually a Western term to describe the pathological forms Islam can take. Like any true religion, Islam itself is basically merciful. For example, the Koran is clear that no Muslim can convert an unbeliever by force. (Jihad is a defensive concept, a means of protecting the faith, not one of conquest.) The traditional poor tax, or *zakat*, establishes a rightful claim of the poor against the assets of the rich. The Koran gives women legal rights that were unprecedented in Muhammad's day. The corrupt, violent, male chauvinist "fundamentalism" that prevails in Sudan today is a perversion of Islamic "fundamentals," not their essence.

I was last in Sudan almost 30 years ago, and I can sense the change in mood since then. I was traveling by third-class railway from Khartoum to the Egyptian border, on my way to see the monuments of Abu Simbel before they were carved up and reassembled above the lake rising behind the new Aswan Dam. (The train trip took 18 hours then; it now takes three days, an index of what has been happening to Sudan.) The Sudanese in my compartment were no less devout than those today – at each stop in the desert, people would climb out and spread mats on the sand for their prayers. But the atmosphere was one of gracefulness and hospitality, not suspicion and fear. Islam in Sudan today has been contaminated for the cynical ends of those in power.

*   *   *

Looking through SUNDOS's founding documents, the mission leader unearths the following nugget:

> The main objective of this project is to strengthen the capacity to prepare for, manage, and monitor the deteriorating drought situation and to facilitate regional planning and disaster preparations in part of the Sudan which, because of environmental trends, is becoming increasingly susceptible to finance.

Just as we thought...

*   *   *

Sunday. I am at one of the local Christian service organizations. (Sunday is a working day in Sudan, though the people I am talking with will knock off early for church.) These are folks who spend every day in the midst of war and drought, digging wells where there is no surface water, getting food to the displaced, helping people in the camps start little shops as a step toward self-reliance.

In areas the war has finally passed by, this group is also trying to help resettle people out of the camps. People start by being suspicious: they have all heard of schemes where the government "resettled" people, gave them seeds to plant and tools to plant them with, fed them until harvest, and then took the crop, leaving them with nothing. Families willing to try anyway are given a small "survival kit" (needle and thread, a bar of soap, matches, two cups and a saucepan, a razor blade, seed and tools, and enough food for three months) and trucked off into the bush to start life over.

As I listen to these stories, I am struck by an extraordinary serenity in the people telling them, faith carried lightly in the midst of awfulness. It takes the form of humility and service, the qualities you somehow expect in people of deep faith, but don't always find.

It makes me happy to come upon this. I have been re-reading C.S. Lewis during my evenings, and have been jolted at the unhumble edge I find in some of his writings this time. I used to like the uncompromising quality of his belief (on the subject of God, no belief should be half-hearted); now I am more aware of the wall of self-satisfaction (too strong a term, but there is something like that at work) that Lewis has built between himself and those who do not share, in his way, his One True Faith. The Christians of Khartoum cannot indulge themselves this way; the tests of their faith are much too urgent.

*　　　　　*　　　　　*

Our report is done, 150 pages on the history and accomplishments (if that is the right word) of SUNDOS. In the U.N. system, evaluation reports tend to have dozens of upbeat recommendations. ("Since the project area is flooded each year by the rains, the government should convene a task force to consider a coordinated interagency response to ensure that water runs uphill during the next project phase.") Our report has two recommendations: (1) terminate SUNDOS at once, and (2) don't do it again. A couple of days' worth of meetings to tell this to UNDP and other interested parties, and we will be through.

*　　　　　*　　　　　*

Done, wrapped and delivered. Still, I am left with the nagging feeling that much has been elusive here. Working on SUNDOS would make one feel that way, of course: wherever we looked, there was no SUNDOS there. But it is more than that. Sudanese are extra-wary of foreigners these days (we are all suspect in the eyes of security), so they have to withhold large parts of themselves. To whom are we talking? When we do talk, the stories get distorted by the charge in the atmosphere. (A Sudanese Christian insists that the Koran endorses conversion by bribery and force; she is wrong, but there is bitter experience behind what she is saying.) I think back on the things I have heard (and have recorded here), and wonder how much I really know of the reality behind them.

In other places I have been in recent years (India, Vietnam), the surface of things has had a lot more definition than this. You always know there is a vast world beyond what you are seeing, but at least there is something distinct to look at. Not in Sudan, not now. I know there is awfulness out there, and heroism and brutality and caring, but I cannot be certain of their shapes.

When we were in El Obeid, one of my field trips took me to El'ain to look at microcatchments (a fancy word for yard-wide circles of sandy earth, banked on the downhill side, that retain enough water when it rains to let you grow trees or grasses there). We drove along one of the state's few tarmac roads, the straight ribbon of it tapering to shimmering heat far ahead of us. For a time, the road ended in watery mirage; then something trembled slightly, the water vanished, *everything* vanished – color, substance – and we were headed for a small patch of nothing, absolute emptiness carved somehow from the day. Then the water shimmered back, and the road; I could not get a fix on what was happening out there. There has been something of that in the whole experience of being in Sudan.

When we did get to El'ain, the microcatchments had washed away. I may not see the shape of things here, but I am beginning to sense patterns. I'm ready to go home.

Chapter 10
ERITREA
MAY-OCTOBER 1995

By 1994, I had been working for the World Food Program for more than eight years. I was becoming increasingly disillusioned with life as a food aid bureaucrat. With good reason, the WFP system had always considered professional assessments of its activities to be a potential hindrance to dumping their food resources in the most expeditious manner. (If anyone had taken seriously the feasibility of WFP's development activities, most of them would have had to be shut down.) Soon after her appointment in 1992, a new Executive Director found a way to resolve this tension, emasculating the technical review group of which I was a part and vastly expanding a public relations staff whose job was to tell the world that all was well with food aid. Toward the end of 1994, the possibility arose of my becoming Country Director of the WFP office in Eritrea. It seemed a way to get back into the real world.

It was 115° in Tessenei when we rolled in last Tuesday afternoon, but it cooled a bit – by eight o'clock or so, at Anna Morris's for dinner, it was an even 100°, where it pretty much stayed through the night. My kind of weather.

I had forgotten how very complex and individual the people in bush towns like Tessenei seem. I don't know whether this is because only the extremely strange end up in such places (I'm not counting the genuine inhabitants) or because you see people more vividly in a context so raw.

Take Anna. Anna is Eritrean, though God knows what passport she travels on by now. Her mother used to work as a cleaner in the mission that is now the Tessenei hospital. One day the Ethiopian army passed through and murdered the mother, and Anna took off walking into the Sudan. She eventually made it to England, where she got married and had a child (now in his twenties and somewhere else). When the marriage broke up, she went to visit a friend in Singapore and ended up spending two years on a ship in the South China Sea rescuing boat people. Most days, she would fly with the helicopter pilot off the ship in search of refugees. Sometimes the Thai navy would try to shoot them down, but the pilot was an American, ex-Vietnam, with a great evade. She says the worst times were finding empty boats, their occupants raped and murdered by pirates or swept overboard in the previous night's storms. At times, though, there was such a euphoria to being on the ship that hitting port again was a tremendous downer, all land-sickness and depression.

When the swings got so bad she had to quit, she spent a year coming down (or getting back up), worked with refugees in Uganda, got somehow to Heidelberg to study pediatric nursing, and convinced the German millionaire whose ship had been picking up the boat people to start a hospital project in Tessenei. Now she's back working in the building where her mother was killed.

If the hospital project folds, as it may, Anna could go anywhere, off to Zaire, back to Europe. She is Eritrean but not Eritrean by now, and everywhere is equally her home, or nowhere. These are the people you meet in places like Tessenei, the saints and whiskey priests and expatriate project managers, the free-lance "journalists" and burnouts, the radically displaced. I don't know why I am so powerfully moved by meeting such people, but I am.

Part of it is the context. We are in no-frills country here, no deodorants and lubricants, the constant abrasion leaving people's edges sticking out so you learn to back off and give them space, just watching what they do. It leads to an exceptional degree of courtesy and respect and clear-sightedness – when the people involved are not hacking each other to death.

You are never quite free of that undertone of violence. There were three decades of war here before Eritrea gained independence from Ethiopia two years ago, and the residue is everywhere. The road between Keren and Tessenei was the escape route for the Ethiopian soldiers fleeing Asmara into Sudan at the end of the war, and all along the way we pass the shells of tanks and lorries that were mined or shelled or torched or otherwise detained.

In a way I have yet to achieve, the Eritreans have come to accept all the debris as part of the environment. I was talking in Agordat with an ex-fighter, pretty gimpy from being shot up during the war, who is running the province's refugee program. As we talked, two little girls jumped into the burned-out shell of a tank nearby. I was about to dig out my camera when I realized they had pulled down their drawers and ducked out of sight to take a leak. Postwar Agordat's version of a municipal *pissoir.*

Not everything from the war has been so effectively recycled. Anna sees a steady trickle of mine victims, and the best estimates are that 300,000-500,000 mines are still out there, waiting for goats or camels or children to step on them.

There are new forms of edginess as well. A few miles north of Agordat, where we spent the last night on the road, the jihad folks shot up a government Land Cruiser a couple of weeks ago, killing the driver and a Water Board engineer. Then they set the thing on fire and burned everyone down to ash. In Tessenei, we met the Nairobi correspondent for the London *Observer* at lunch in the Luna Hotel. He had just been visiting Eritrean refugee camps in the Sudan, where the terrorists-in-training were celebrating the incident as a great event. Nobody expects it to be the last.

The fundamentalists feed on the frustrations and poverty of the largely Muslim lowlands, problems that are not going to go away. Twenty thousand Eritrean refugees have been repatriated from Sudan through Tessenei since November, and another 100,000-200,000 are expected in the next year or two, mostly to be settled in the low-lands. There are a lot of jagged edges here: the refugees are moved into settlements only meagerly supplied with the housing and schools and clinics they had been promised, the next wave of refugees will overwhelm the government's resources and receive even less, and the original residents are resentful at not getting anything from all this except competition for their fuelwood and water supplies.

At the same time, there is a lot of resilience at work. We drove from one settlement to the land its people will start farming in the next month or two. It is a six-mile commute each way, but gangs of people were digging trees out of the ground and getting the fields ready to plant. When they found we were travelling with someone from the Ministry of Agriculture, they tried to convince him to build a diversion channel to bring water from the river to their fields. They won't get their channel, but they should be okay if the rains come. If not...

If not, the World Food Program (me) and the Eritrean Relief and Rehabilitation Agency (ERRA) spring into action. WFP delivers a couple of hundred thousand tons of food to Massawa. ERRA takes the food from Massawa to villages around the country (WFP pays the freight). Both of our organizations are very good at doing these things.

Anna deals with other aspects of poverty. Before we left Tessenei, she took us on a tour of her hospital. People were lying on cots or mats spread on the ground, relatives fanning them or wiping the sweat from their faces, brushing away flies, in many cases just waiting for them to die. (Someone later used a phrase to describe the mayor of Tessenei – "gently hopeless" – that could equally apply to these relatives of the sick.) There was a man with a "suspicious condition" (i.e., AIDS), a bunch of women with acute anemia after childbirth (if you peel an eyelid down, it is chalky white inside), the inevitable child with severe burns from falling into his mother's fire, a young woman all skeleton from some wasting condition ("She is going to die," said Anna), some-one in his second day of coma from cerebral malaria ("He'll probably make it"), a man with a softball-sized tumor in his belly waiting for Friday's round of surgery. Anna talks with them all, touches them, leaves behind a little eddy of reassurance.

These are the human symptoms of a pathology of poverty and hunger, just as the structural food gap figures are the statistical symptoms. What I keep trying to do is wed all these levels of abstraction and concreteness, find some wholeness of thought and experience, create the right eddies. I haven't expressed this well in the paragraphs above, but I know what I am looking for. And I am infinitely grateful for the chance to do it here.

*　　　　　*　　　　　*

Out in the countryside, looking at watersheds and resettlement camps, there is a sense of openness, of expanding skies. Here in Asmara, there is a sense of compression, of spinning faster and faster in some kind of vortex. The kind of fatigue you get at the end of a day in the field feels healthy, your muscles tired and your head full of images. I'm not so sure about the fatigue you get at the end of weeks of urban compression, your heart beating too fast and your head full of noise, the way I feel today.

Still, I would a thousand times rather be in Asmara than back in Rome. For one thing, there is so much new and unchosen to life. If I had actually *planned* my post-Rome career, I would never have thought of many of the things that occupy me here: Massawa port and stevedoring charges, the advisability of fortified cereal blends as a ration for returnees from the Sudan, payment modalities for transporting commodities to Extended Delivery Points (flat rate? payment against bills of lading?), the best way to word an EMOP amendment so that ERRA can monetize 6,000 tons of our wheat through the flour mills, some of the details of running the office (should we fly a consultant down from Addis [why not bring Alex from Dublin?] to get us on email and make us a LAN?). These are things I cannot do from memory, and I love the zest of that.

Even the things I know a lot about have very different resonance in a context like this. I've brought one consultant in from the States to look at natural resource management and someone else to deal with issues relating to food security (food aid planning and monitoring, monetization, early warning systems, vulnerability mapping). And

I'm contracting with social scientists here in town to look at targeting of food aid at the village level. I have spent big chunks of the last few years in Rome thinking more or less abstractly about things like these, but the idea now is to build a specific, five-year program for WFP's work in Eritrea – we are talking about millions of dollars worth of aid – and the issues could hardly seem more real and tangible and challenging.

Then there is the stuff that (for better or worse) fits around the edges: the evening *passeggiata* through the *centro*, the representational duties of a Head of Agency (watching the Independence festivities from the V.I.P. box at Asmara Stadium, drinking midday Prosecco with the Italians on their National Day, marching behind the President in the funeral cortege for one of the greatest heroes of the struggle for liberation), the round of semi-social, semi-official functions with the usual suspects (David and Becky from Catholic Relief Services, Ephraim and Dr. Nerayo from ERRA, Anne and Barbel and Jackie and Karin and Barbara, Ato Gerense, Bram and Hinnie from Lutheran World Federation, Asmarom Legesse, the UN refugee agency's Arnulf and his friend Peter, various ambassadors and ex-fighters and Italian teachers and government officials and expatriate volunteers).

All these disparate clusters of things, somehow getting done. No wonder the feeling of zest and exhilaration, of (on good days) mastery – *I can do this!* – a reminder of times long ago when just being able to do something new was life enough (watch any kid learning to turn cartwheels).

But you can also lose your way (and cartwheel into a tree). For the first couple of years in Malawi, I felt the way I feel here now. Then I realized that while I had been doing things, something had gotten fundamentally off-center in my relationship with my family, with my colleagues, with Malawi itself; and the next years were pretty close to hell. I don't want to go through that again.

I suspect that the sense of zest and mastery can be a kind of experiential fool's gold, a lure down a slippery path, and that the sense of compression and noise is a warning. What do I do about it?

Watch this space.

*　　　　　*　　　　　*

Anne Callanan is my right hand in the WFP office here. She's one of the people who have been through the really hard times in humanitarian aid, participating in relief efforts during times of famine and war in places like Ethiopia, Somalia, Pakistan, Burundi, Uganda, and Iraq.

In 1984, for example, she was working in refugee camps during the worst famine in Ethiopian history. Here's what it was like for her:

> I was remembering last night the drive down from Kombolcha at 5:00 every morning to the camp, and how we used to brace ourselves going around that last bend in the road before entering what we called the valley of death. It was so cold, and there was always a pall of smoke over the camp, what could be imagined as the breath of the 20,000 people living there. In the early morning, our ritual was to check the shelters for those who had died in the night. One morning, I had two beautiful babies in a cardboard box waiting to be buried, one I had found on the ground. There's a woman who haunts me still. We had a measles epidemic and many children died. All the children used to have plastic armbands. Do you remember the hairnets Ethiopian women used to wear? Well, this woman came up to me and undid knots in her hairnet, and inside were five armbands, she had lost everything. I still see the agony on her face.

There are unknown numbers of people who lived because Anne was there, but she doesn't see it that way. For her, "The thing is, you don't think about the ones who lived; you only remember the ones who died. And that's where it hangs, because you can't feel proud about anything when you've seen so many people dying." Bearing witness at times like that is an act of grace in itself, though, and Anne has been one of the witness bearers.

*   *   *

The pennies are beginning to drop: the longer I stay, the more I see that our aid (and that of other major donors, such as the European Union) has fallen into patterns that are not entirely healthy. We have flooded the country with so much grain that its price in local markets has been driven to record lows. It becomes difficult for farmers to make a living. And the process reinforces itself. We have to give people in our development projects food worth the amount of a daily wage. Since food has little value, we have to provide several times the normal amount for a day's work. Workers can't use that much food, so private traders come to the distribution points, buy it from them as they're receiving it, and take it back to urban markets, further depressing its price.

There's much more going wrong. Food intended for Eritrea's needy gets trucked illegally across the border into Ethiopia, where prices for it are higher, and sold there. Some ends up at the flour mills, which make cheap bread for distribution to potentially restive urban dwellers, not what we had in mind. Our payments to ERRA for moving food around are way beyond the actual cost of transport, leaving excess cash that the government uses for other things. To keep the food flowing that provides all these benefits, there is every incentive to fiddle a number or two: the population figures are jacked up, estimates of food production and reserves are jacked down, the food gap grows (on paper) and must be filled (at the port). It creates an environment where obfuscation and sleight-of-hand become increasingly necessary, at a time when you could argue instead for clarity of vision and transparency of action.

I remind myself of the context within which all this is happening. Eritrea had been gobbled up by Ethiopia after World War II. In 1961, Eritreans began to resist, small groups that the Ethiopians called "shiftas" (bandits) challenging the Ethiopian army. Gradually, the shiftas became an independence movement that fought off a vastly superior Ethiopian military that had total control of the air and massive materiel support from the Soviet Union. It took 30 years of often-brutal struggle; but in 1961, the Ethiopians conceded defeat. In a referendum in 1993, Eritreans voted all but unanimously for independence. It's only two years later now, meaning that the country has a powerfully lingering wartime mentality. The people running things are used to shooting their way through problems, not thinking their way through.

*   *   *

If the people at the top are used to winning battles, the people at the bottom are used to losing them. As in Ethiopia, you everywhere see folks wearing the kinds of clothes that arrive in bales from humanitarian groups in the U.S. and Europe. The children especially pick through the bales in search of the drabbest clothing they can find – they're terrified by the thought that anything colorful could make them visible to the Ethiopian fighter jets they're used to being strafed by. I can't imagine what their dreams must be like. Surely there's a way for food aid to bring healing to the children. I'll have to find someone who can figure out how to do that.

*   *   *

Troubling signs of the government's sense of embattlement. The current *Eritrea Profile* reports on "President Isaias's reply to questions from the public." Among other comments, the President is quoted as saying:

> – (re ex-members of the Eritrean Liberation Front, an opposition group) We know who is who, but we prefer to let sleeping dogs lie, otherwise it would be very easy for us to open the books and settle matters one by one.
> – (on regional restructuring) This question has already been clarified by the responsible body and if it is still not very clear it is only because some people would not accept it and are trying to spread their distorted views. Such biased thinking is a legacy of colonialism, created along the lines of divide-and-rule.
> – (on the Press Code) In this country everyone is free to express his or her opinions. As there is no problem on that score, it remains only to make the matter official and then the hotheads will be satisfied.

Any volunteers to be the first to freely express an opinion?

*   *   *

Uh-oh. Barbara, the European Union's food aid person, just rang. The Ministry of Foreign Affairs called in the EU Delegate yesterday and told him he has a choice: either the EU gets Barbara out of the country or Government declares her persona non grata (PNG). They apparently tried to hint at irregularities in her personal lifestyle, but nobody is going to believe that shit. Her only offense has been in taking the lead (with me close behind) in spotting the ways our food aid has gone astray.

Recall the President on the Press Code: "In this country everyone is free to express his or her opinions. As there is no problem on that score, it remains only to make the matter official and then the hot-heads will be satisfied."

As I said, what "hothead" is going to volunteer to be the first to speak out? Barbara did, honestly and constructively, and look what is happening to her.

As the boys in *Spinal Tap* pointed out, there is a fine line between stupid and clever. Stupid: this would be the end of the Eritrea Myth (the steadfast determination of all those brave and honest fighters for freedom and justice), with large consequences for the kind of continuing support that could be expected from outside. Clever: they could give us the finger, PNG Barbara, trot out Jacky Sutton (a stringer for the BBC) to file stories about hollow-bellied babies, and find the world pouring in food aid on their usual terms. Which is it to be?

Whatever, we can make a pretty good guess as to who will be PNGed next.

*   *   *

Hollow laughter. Arnulf, the acting head of the UN system in Eritrea, stopped by yesterday to inform me that the Minister of Foreign Affairs had called him in last Thursday – the same day the EU Delegate was called in about Barbara – and told him that the UN should get me out of the country or I would be PNGed. The charges:

(1) that I had "questioned the integrity of the Government", and (2) that I was "biased about the solutions to Eritrea's problems…"

Words to live by: "We know who is who, but we prefer to let sleeping dogs lie, otherwise it would be very easy for us to open the books and settle matters one by one" (Isaias Afwerki, President of Eritrea, talking about the ELF). Wake up, sleeping dogs!

*   *   *

The story is beginning to get around Asmara, so I called a staff meeting to let my folks know before they heard it elsewhere. I said that the Ministry of Foreign Affairs was asking me to leave the country, but they shouldn't worry about their own positions because the Minister had made it clear that Government very much values WFP (if not its present Country Director). It all took about two minutes.

I couldn't have foreseen how shattering it would be for me. As I was doing my spiel, I looked around the room at the people I'd been working with. Aregash was clearly stunned; Dawit looked as if he was going to cry; everybody was reacting in one degree or another. I realized how much connection there was between us all, the unity in the room. Maybe nobody else saw it quite that way, but I suddenly felt how it was *true*.

I also felt the good patterns that we increasingly, together, have been gestating and making peek from behind clouds and spinning off in right moments of connection with the people we deal with, the promise for Eritrea in this – all lost now. I feel awful.

The world is controlled by evil people, full of death; what is amazing is the extent to which love and connection prevail among us anyway as we move through the day.

*   *   *

Last night's word is that I am expected to leave the country within ten days. Barbara leaves next Friday, [niece] Maria [who had been staying with me] on Monday night, [brother] Douglas won't be coming at all.

At least we all had more warning than Glenn Anders and Kurt Walters, the U.S. Agency for International Development representative and his deputy. They got called in on Monday afternoon and were told they were leaving Tuesday. Something about AID bringing someone in for a short visit without having gotten the paperwork fully completed on his airport visa; it happens all the time, but in this case the Deputy Minister of Interior decided to toss out the whole AID office. Even that was better than what he did to the airport staffers who had let the guy in through immigration; he tossed *them* into jail.

Jacky Sutton appears to be an intermediate case: just before she left a couple of weeks ago for a visit to the U.K., she was told she wasn't going to be allowed back into the country.

This is one of the strangest times of my life. Every third conversation since this all began has involved somebody passing on the latest news to someone else and getting the reaction "................... .... *what?* .... " Nobody can believe any of this is happening. We talk about little else, I suppose hoping that by repetition of what we know we might stumble onto an explanation; but it hasn't worked yet. At least we have figured out the stages people invariably seem to go through in dealing with it: shock, denial, anger, acceptance, packing. Anne will have to tidy up after me.

*   *   *

Now I'm *really* pissed off. The Voice of America, the BBC, Radio Deutsche Welle, and Radio Vatican reported yesterday that "two American aid workers [Anders and Walters] and two other aid workers have been expelled from Eritrea for 'interference in the country's internal affairs.'" *Two other aid workers!* – some weeks you just get no damn respect at all.

Add Isaias watch: The most recent *Economist* to arrive here has an interview with the president on the subject of Sudan. (Sudan is one of those other problems without which everything would be perfect in Free Eritrea.) Isaias minces no words: "We are out to see that this government is not there any more. We are not trying to pressure them to talk to us, or to behave in a more constructive way. We will give weapons to anyone committed to overthrowing them."

. . . .

.. *what?* . . . . This is simply not how rational heads of state talk. Poor Isaias: "We have tried to develop some sort of partnership. But our goodwill has been abused." Right; shoot them. I'm glad I'm just getting PNGed....[7]

---

[7] While I was in Eritrea, people perceived as dissidents were being consigned to an underground prison in Asmara and sometimes tortured to death. (A government cabinet minister was reputed to enjoy the process enough that he'd do the torturing himself.) More recently, a U.N. commission of inquiry found that Eritrean government officials currently engage in extrajudicial executions, torture, forced labor, rape and sexual servitude, all in the context of "a total lack of rule of law." The Committee to Protect Journalists considers Eritrea the world's "most censored country," with North Korea coming second. Hundreds of thousands of Eritreans have fled the country. Getting PNGed was an act of mercy.

TRAVELS WITH DAVID

Chapter 11

ANGOLA

1996-97

After being tossed out of Eritrea, I took five months of recuperative but unpaid "holiday" in the U.S. Being PNGed is the kiss of death for a career within the United Nations system, and I wondered what WFP would find for me to do next. For my sins, they posted me to one of the worst places in the world, Angola on the trailing edge of a civil war.

It would be reassuring to hear a single nice word about Angola. In my briefing by Personnel, Patricia explained cheerfully that in the system WFP uses to classify its offices, Angola is categorized as a "hellhole." Beverley told me about someone who was recently there and who had water in his taps twice in the course of the month. (He apparently bathed in bottled water, when there was any.) This may have been the period when Reuters was reporting a lapse in water supply in Luanda since somebody had vandalized the electrical pylons to get metal for window frames, shutting down the electricity, the pumping system, and the water. Or it may simply be that Luanda is always without water. Beverley started to tell an even better Angola story, and then caught herself and changed the subject.

As for the electricity, there seems not to be any. The last email from Paul, one of the people I'll be working with, mentioned that his generator had driven his neighbors crazy, so he was having to move. In such a situation, I gather, your option is to sit in candlelight and watch the sweat pour off yourself onto the floor. (Luanda weather is apparently 100 degrees and 100% humidity day and night all year, except in the summer when it gets hot.) According to Paul, everybody is hoping they'll get one of the turbines fixed so there will be electricity at least some of the time.

To give people a chance to let off tension, Reuters says there are 100,000 AK-47s in private hands in Luanda. (You can buy your own for $50 or so.) Paul made some offhand observation about how life in the bush is better than life in town since at least you can walk around, which you can't in Luanda. One can more or less guess why not.

I suppose Paul meant you can walk around in the bush if you know where you're walking. According to the May *Scientific American*, there are 15 million land mines out there waiting for someone to pass by, 50% more than in Cambodia, 15 times as many as in Eritrea, third behind Egypt and Iran (would you have guessed?) in the global Big Leagues of land mines. Beverley almost had me buying into the "Accidental Death or Dismemberment" policy WFP offers until I found that among the policy's "exclusions" are deaths or injuries "caused directly by war, whether declared or not, or any act of war, or insurrection," which is to say those deaths or injuries you're most likely to suffer in Angola. Just gotta watch your feet, I guess.

Another reason to watch your feet is what you might see if you looked up. Nobody knows how many AK-47s remain in rural hands, but a couple were used last month to blow away two passing U.N. types and an OXFAM honcho out for a drive in the Angolan countryside. And Angola is not a place to have major (or minor) medical problems: the doctors at Luanda's main hospital (all three of them?) went on strike recently because their $5 monthly salary hadn't been paid and the hospital lacked both medicines and (naturally) running water.

Food seems to be a problem too, according to Valerie, who (as WFP's Regional Manager for West Africa) should know. Even if you had water to cook in and electricity to do the cooking, she says, you might not find food to cook in Luanda. And we're talking here about the employees of a food aid agency; imagine what life is like for everyone else.

That is just the physical comfort/survival side of things. A friend of a friend tried to work in Angola recently and says there is simply no government to work with. That may not be entirely true; others claim that there is lots of government there, all with hands (and AK-47s) out to get their cut of the food aid. Whatever, my job description requires me to ensure that "contacts are established/maintained with... relevant Government departments in order to establish priority sectors" so as to "define a strategy for WFP assistance in [Angola's] reconstruction/ rehabilitation phase." It looks like something of a challenge to find the departments with which to establish/maintain contacts, much less to strategize with.

I know, I know, it's just like everywhere, the world is precarious, *la vita è sempre dura e difficile*, work is tough, no big deal. Except that when I went to get my transfer letter from Beverley today, I found that among my entitlements is "Rest and Recuperation: one calendar week for every two months worked, to be taken in Windhoek or Sao Tome." We food aid bureaucrats are tough sorts; I've never heard of a post where you get R&R every two months, and in Windhoek or Sao Tome? What have I gotten myself into this time?

*　　　　　*　　　　　*

I've been in Luanda now long enough to look around. I don't think I got grossly misbriefed on my way out here. The Meridien Presidente manages to keep itself (mostly) in water and electricity, but those are things you cannot count on in the real world outside. The process of finding a livable apartment at reasonable cost sounds grimmer every day, but when the alternative is to pay $150 a night[8] for the Presidente, my expectations should rapidly adapt.

Expenses in general seem as if they might be a challenge. At a modest lunch with my new colleague Felix, the bill for two came to 4.2 million Kwanza. The really alarming thing is that in real money, that still amounts to $40 or so. (Life here is not going to be cheap.) But even after all the adjustments are made, inflation of this magnitude has consequences of its own. At the end of the day, I stopped by the "supermarket" to get some bottled water. The woman ahead of me

---

[8] That was in 1996 prices. The same room now goes for more than $300 a night. The cost of items such as meals and rents has probably also doubled since 1996.

paid for her bag of groceries with a stack of bills 1,400 deep (we all counted them with her). Half an hour later, she probably would have needed 1,600.

To keep things interesting, everybody has great stories about the security situation: the police and the army shot it out across the street from the WFP office a few weeks ago (nobody injured); an expat got killed walking out the front door of her apartment building into a firefight between guards and a couple of carjackers; somebody from one of the nongovernmental organizations (NGOs) had to take some heavily armed robbers home to fetch serious money when they found he had too little with him on the street; everyone paled when I suggested I might cross the street from the hotel to stroll on the beach after dinner. Especially at night, we go out only in groups, like the Russians in Africa during Soviet days. And we go everywhere with our two-way radios. "Whiskey Papa," I say into my radio, "this is Lima 9, under attack." The theory is that Whiskey Papa sends reinforcements, but I don't want to have to find out if it really works.

Everybody says that things are much worse than they were during the war, since a million or so extra people have moved into Luanda, the government has stopped paying its workers, and many of the wartime food distribution points have been shut down. The result is total desperation among countless Angolans, who are apparently ready to accept (or perpetuate) any kind of violence to escape the present state of hopelessness. The idea of a coup d'état arises in every discussion, though nobody seems quite sure whose coup it would be, or with what result.

To illustrate the potential for irony in the outcome, consider how Angola got here in the first place. The civil war was Jonas Savimbi's creation, with massive support from the U.S. and the apartheid-era South Africans. Having lost the shooting war plus the elections that followed, Savimbi is now (rather slowly) integrating his forces into the Angolan army. One vaguely plausible scenario would have the Savimbi wing then stage a coup from "inside," giving him power after all. People more and more are asking, why not?; what have we got to lose?

Who are the good guys and who are the bad guys? President dos Santos is in France now. The official reason is that he is having a medical checkup; the unofficial explanation is that he is preparing his "refuge," à la Baby Doc in flight from Haiti. But surely dos Santos isn't just another Mobutu or Duvalier? you ask; the response is a gentle smile, you're still fresh off the plane.

He would not be the only one doing well by doing bad here. In its usual delicate fashion, the World Bank recently reported that: "Income distribution in Angola is extremely skewed... [W]ell-placed people in the oil and military sectors enjoy high living standards." Protocol forbids mention of senior government officials, but everyone understands. My favorite officialdom story so far has to do with the governor ("owner" is the term people actually use) of Malanje Province. Among other things, the governor had cornered the salt trade in Malanje. When WFP started to include salt in its emergency rations, he announced that he could no longer "guarantee the safety" of WFP's representative in Malanje. She was on the next plane out of the country, and salt continued to be a monopoly of the governor's. A trivial incident, but with a certain illustrative power.

Eventually, I suppose the question has to arise: what is WFP doing in a place like this? Felix's fast answer is well, we can't change the government, but we can try to reach people in need. That is WFP's answer in like situations everywhere, but I am not certain I find it adequate. On the other hand, to visibly find it inadequate would probably get me PNGed again. How very tiresome that would be. Stay tuned for developments.

*   *   *

Perhaps strangest of all is the degree to which you can ignore all these realities. If I wanted, I could pretty much move between two fortresses – the Meridien Presidente and the office – separated by a forgettable three-minute walk. In the office, I could spend my time on email, that alternative space where everyone you know hangs out. At the hotel, I could read and watch CNN. I could be anywhere and nowhere, but certainly not in Angola.

CNN is a homogenizing phenomenon almost too strange to report. You can walk down the corridors of almost any international hotel in the world and not miss a word – every room you pass has the channel at top volume. Every fifteen minutes they run a half-hour of business news, Larry King is on constantly, and they keep you from falling asleep by breaking up the monotony with special features. This morning's was a Special Travel Advisory. "Want tips on how to find a good restaurant in a strange city?" some overwired hack was shouting. "First, look in local guidebooks! Second, ask people who live in the city! Third, when you get there, order the food the restaurant is known for! This has been a Special CNN Travel Advisory!" CNN is like the word processor – how did we ever survive before it was invented?

*   *   *

Angola can break your heart, I suspect. Of all the slaves taken from Africa over the centuries, something like 30% came from here. When the Portuguese got out of simple slaving and got into really settling the place, they kept the Africans around largely for servants, sex, and forced labor on the coffee plantations. After an often bloody, 14-year independence struggle (air bombardments, napalmed villages, the whole cookie), 90% of the Portuguese abruptly left, carrying with them everything of value that was portable and destroying the rest. The Russians and Cubans and South Africans and Americans took over from there, arming one Angolan faction or another to fight capitalism or communism or the Namibians (whose independence forces operated from southern Angola) or maybe just their own demons. Nearly 20 years of civil war killed half a million people and left 70,000 (mostly civilians) limbless or otherwise maimed. And it's not over yet:

> A major problem that will plague any effort to rehabilitate the agricultural sector is the widespread and indiscriminate sowing of land mines that took place during more than three decades of anticolonial and civil war. Most mines were buried on footpaths leading either to rivers where people (mostly women and children) obtain water or to small agricultural plots used for subsistence farming. Land mines

were placed by 10 separate armies, including the
Portuguese, the MPLA, UNITA, the Frente Nacional
de Libertação de Angola (FNLA), Cuba, Zaire, South
Africa, the South West Africa People's Organization
(SWAPO), the African National Congress (ANC), and
various armed factions of the Frente de Libertação
do Enclave de Cabinda. It is estimated that there are
10 million of these mines [Scientific American says
15 million] in all – roughly one per Angolan citizen
– and maps for less than 20 percent of them. (Shawn
H. McCormick, *The Angolan Economy: Prospects for
Growth in a Postwar Environment*)

Clearly, there are lot of bad guys in the picture, and not just the
Westerners whose wet dreams over the centuries have had Angola as
a backdrop. Somebody today described the President, Eduardo dos
Santos, and his UNITA adversary, Jonas Savimbi, as fighting to occupy
the moral low ground, brothers in social unconsciousness. Oil reve-
nues (which dos Santos controls) bring in $4 billion a year; diamond
exports (much of which Savimbi controls) are worth at least another
$500 million annually. Absolutely everyone agrees that none of this
reaches the 99% of the population who are struggling to survive. The
other 1% – how does the World Bank put it? – therefore "enjoy high
living standards": do the arithmetic.

The signs are everywhere. The percentage of children in primary
schools is only three-fifths the rate elsewhere in Africa. Even so, there
are so few schools that the average classroom has 90 students. In many
rural communities, a recent donors' conference was told, the primary
education system has simply ceased to function. The mortality rate
for children under five is twice the African average, while the World
Bank characterizes governmental spending on primary health care
as "negligible."

I keep being told that the people in the countryside hardly care
anymore about the missing schools and clinics; they just want to be
left alone. Not a chance. Even in today's "peacetime" conditions, provincial officials and semi-demobilized soldiers get their own piece of

the action by playing games with food aid, imposing "tolls" on people traveling the roads, or waiting until crops are harvested and then taking them at gunpoint.

A story. After the Bicesse Accord in 1991, people believed the war was really over. Refugees began to return from places like Zambia and Zaire, and people left the towns where they had been holed up and returned to their land. An agronomist I spoke with visited an area that had been abandoned for years and found people planting maize under the remains of the coffee trees. "It couldn't work," said the agronomist. "Maize needs more sun than that, and they had no fertilizer to compensate, and yet there were whole hillsides of tall, strong maize plants. I'm embarrassed to say it, but I have to think that they planted their maize not in fertilizer, but in hope."

Then Savimbi lost the election, the fighting started all over again, and the maize never got harvested. The two years that followed were the bloodiest of the entire war.

* * *

The question nags on: What are the aid agencies doing in a place that is awash with oil and diamonds, the proceeds from which go into the overseas accounts of a few generals and politicos? Why are we putting our millions into paying Angola's social bills, while billions are being slurped up by the pigs at the trough?

Always the Gemini, I have conflicting inclinations. Part of me thinks that societies should do what they reasonably can before asking for help. Since nothing like that is happening here, we should go elsewhere and let the Angolans sort themselves out.

The problem with this is that it assumes "the Angolans" are some sort of whole, with sorting mechanisms in place to achieve the common good. But there is no whole. Rather, society here consists of two unrelated entities: the Pigs and the People. The Pigs have all the money, and the People have whatever land they can clear in the midst of the mines. As if in some science fiction novel, these entities inhabit the same space without ever seeing each other. It is not that having the aid agencies here lets the Pigs avoid their duty to the People; the

Pigs don't even know the People are there. For the agencies to pull out would simply hurt the People, without in any way getting the Pigs' attention or changing the way they do things. So we stay?

Things get more complex from there. I have been describing the short run; there is also a long run. Some argue that continuing to help the People simply postpones the day when the Pigs have to rethink their position or get bounced. Better to stop providing palliatives and bring that day forward. So we go?

Maybe, but I was taught at Harvard's Kennedy School (so it must have been right) that Pig-bouncing takes place when people have just a little bit of a better life, can therefore visualize a better life still, and so set out to conquer it. People with nothing at all lack both the energy and the sense of possibility to bounce their Pigs. If this theory is correct, the palliatives of the aid agencies might in fact create the conditions where change is more likely to occur. So we stay?

This in turn assumes that what the agencies do is, at least, of some small benefit to the People. In many countries, however, the trough at which the Pigs dine is full of foreign aid, and the people get hardly the scraps. In these countries, it is hard to imagine any rationale for continuing the aid. So we go?

Is Angola itself such a place? I don't know yet. A lot of unsalaried provincial governors seem to live very well, and aid has to be an important source of their income. Still, a lot of aid gets through to the People, and a lot of them – hundreds of thousands, surely – are alive today only because of this. So we stay?

But that may change. The aid that gets through in quantities sufficient to make a difference tends to be emergency aid, the food we fly into areas under siege from armies or brown with drought. God and Savimbi willing, those days are now past in Angola, and we are moving to the kinds of "reconstruction" and "development" aid that come in much smaller amounts and accomplish little or nothing. This kind of aid will hardly give people the sense of hope to conquer their destinies and bounce the Pigs from their lives. Maybe what we've done here so far has been worthy, but that period is largely over. So we go?

These problems are difficult enough in themselves. Trying to sort them out is made tougher by the fact that the livelihoods and pensions of most everyone I know (not excepting me) depend on continuing to work in places like this. So whatever the merits of the case, we presumably stay...?

Maybe I'll flip a coin.

*   *   *

Luanda curves out into the ocean and back toward the north, like a J, giving protection to the ships docked here. The oceanside leg of the J is lined with hotels and restaurants. On the mainland side, the road we call the Marginal separates a narrow strip of beach from what appears (from my 21st-floor window at the Presidente) to be a Mediterranean holiday town, shops and cafes and apartments, plus a pink confection with columns and dome that could be the casino (but turns out to be the Central Bank, much the same thing here). A wooded hill rises gently from the waterfront to an area of shops and old Portuguese villas. In the evening, with the air soft and the sun setting into the ocean, you can imagine this place as it should be, lovely and serene.

Look more closely. Beneath the double row of palm trees lining the beach are only the street boys whose turf this is and dense scatterings of trash. There is more trash in the streets and in the courtyards, on the roofs of the crumbling buildings, everywhere. The shops and cafes haven't been open in years. The streets are so potholed that in parts of town you need your four-wheel drive. Every third person seems to be carrying an automatic weapon. (Sign outside the supermarket: "PROIBIR ENTRAR ARMADO" – leave your guns outside.) At night, I can sometimes hear gunfire at the port; the next day, boys line the streets with car radios for sale in their original boxes.

And they weren't kidding about this being a city without water. Even the Presidente has run dry, so I really did get to bathe in a liter of bottled water before going to dinner at Paul's last night. Today they say the water is "coming," but they said that yesterday too. At least we still have bottled water. You see people on the streets trying to wash in the dribble condensing off someone's second-floor air conditioner. During the season of heavy nighttime rains, women come out at 4:00

in the morning to do their washing in the water that collects in the ruts in the roads; I can't imagine how they are managing now.

*   *   *

I'm in my new flat. The view out the back is a trickle of sewage and a pile of metal containers meant to be shipping goods across the sea. (What are they doing here?) The view out the front is a heap of well-picked-over trash. The elevators stopped working long ago, and the glass has been stolen from their doors, so a misstep on the landing means you plunge down the shaft. The biggest rats I have ever seen dash across the dirt strip where people park their cars. My own personal guard meets me when I get home and escorts me to my flat; then he spends the night in front of my door and walks me to my car in the morning.

That is outside. Inside is a perfectly adequate space, newly painted, but with certain limitations. The past twenty-four hours, for example, there has been no electricity. No electricity means no pump and therefore no water; it also means no air conditioning (so you sit in candlelight and watch the sweat pour off yourself onto the floor). Sewer gas churns in great bubbles out of the toilet and filters through the flat. Cockroaches that would give the rats a fair fight emerge from nowhere and disappear into nowhere. Food sits gently rotting in the warm fridge. Clothes that got halfway through the wash cycle before the power blew hang heavily on the line.

I am paying $1200 a month for the place, and nobody can believe what a great deal I got.

*   *   *

Posted on the bulletin board at World Vision: "Please listen PASSIVELY to the [two-way] radio. Attend only if necessary, avoid private talks and confidential things. Attend calls for World Vision, telephone colleagues in the event of crisis (shooting, accidents and confusions)."

It is a strange state of mind we inhabit here...

*   *   *

Do I give the impression I think this is a terrible place to be? I tell you solemnly, I think no such thing. This is a terrible place in many ways (all right, in most ways), but that does not mean it is terrible to be here.

There is a kind of crazy grace to being in a place like this. Nothing is easy, nothing can be taken for granted. In an entirely different context, Stephen Levine talks about the way we should always be poised to respond to life: "In the moment where response is called upon, there are no answers that can be carried from one moment to the next. Clear-eyed and open-hearted, we sense from moment to moment what we must do." In a place like Angola, you *have* to proceed through the day clear-eyed and open-hearted. To try to carry your answers with you would only drive you mad. It is a gift to be forced to live like this.

*   *   *

When Savimbi restarted the war in 1992, his forces rapidly occupied a number of provincial capitals, including Huambo (where I am today). The government then took those towns back. Somebody with the right kind of eye could look around this place and reconstruct what happened during that period. To me, it makes no sense at all. There are dozens of gouges the size of a baby's fist in the cement walls of every house, seemingly the spray from a thousand thousand AK-47s. (But why? These were not military targets, and the bullets seldom made it through the walls, just somebody's reminder that he was here.) That is the background noise; the signs of violence and death move sharply upward from there, holes in walls the size of saucers, the size of tables, the size of boxcars, walls tumbled across their foundations – I cannot imagine what weapons accounted for what I am seeing. (And why? These were markets, churches, random houses, what was the point?) It is as if somebody had given an army a year's supply of ammunition, pointed them at Huambo, and told them they had twenty-four hours to expend every round. At the end of the day, the town was saved...

ANGOLA

That was 1992; a lower-grade version of the madness continues today. Driving from Bailundo to Huambo on Tuesday, I ask how security is in Huambo Province these days. Paolo, the man I'm traveling with, says oh, a HALO Trust demining vehicle was ambushed three days ago, a couple of people are in hospital with bullet wounds, nobody killed though. Oh, say I, where was this? A couple of miles down the road, says Paolo; I'll show you the place. And he does.

At the Catholic Relief Services house where I stayed last night, everyone had stories of their own. Ed and Jodie told a corrosively funny series of tales about the night they spent in the stairwell of the CRS house in Cubal while UNITA shelled the town. The worst part, according to Jodie, was when the rats got spooked by the noise and began climbing all over them in panic.

It doesn't go away. Yesterday in Cubal, an armed band of UNITA soldiers (or government soldiers, or bandits, or some combination of the above – nobody is ever quite sure) took over an area and robbed everyone of their chickens and goats. Then they broke into the mission compound where the sisters were staying and scared everyone half to death before taking off with their newly-acquired livestock.

And then, always, there are the mines. Michelle, the Uruguayan doctor who stays at the CRS house here, had to deal with an eleven-year-old the other day whose leg had been blown off. To cut down on such incidents, CRS sponsors a mine awareness program for children. Eileen showed me the dummy mines they use when they talk to the kids. They also give a puppet show. One of the puppets has a detachable leg, and when he steps on a mine he and his leg get hurled in different directions across the stage. Then the children do role-playing, acting out being blown up.

In spite of it all, one of the things I notice everywhere I go in Angola is how much the children sing.

*   *   *

How useful is WFP in the midst of all this? That is what I went touring to see, but I am far from certain of the answer. Paolo took me to a collective farm in Huambo where we are providing food to workers to expand their irrigation facilities. This may be the last collective farm in the world, and it might be worth keeping alive as a museum to a concept now universally discredited. To pump resources into it as a form of agricultural development, though, is something that of all the world's donors, only – literally only – WFP would support.

As we left, the collective's chairman gave Paolo a basket of cabbages and a chicken. Then we all shook hands and professed mutual admiration and undying love. I don't see us getting out of this one anytime soon.

There is a kind of dreaminess that gets us into these things in the first place. On Friday's plane back, one of the people involved in food aid here was telling me about the activities he hopes to support during the reconstruction period. It was like being caught up in an acid flashback, plunged howling yet again into the mindset of the bureaucracy. This is a man of quiet good will, but as he explained what was going through his head, it came out like this:

> (1) Education in Angola is in trouble: schools are typically on three shifts, with few teachers and an average classroom size of 90 students.
> (2) WFP should help education in Angola: we should provide meals for children in the schools, in order to increase attendance and enrolment.

He is not alone in seeing the world this way; as I have too much cause to know, a majority of WFP staff members live all the time with this kind of cognitive dissonance.

*   *   *

Back from a trip to Lobito and Benguela, looking mostly at feeding kitchens and preschool centers in the bairros (Portuguese for slums).

Most of the kitchens weren't working (the electricity was off at the mill where they grind the flour, there was no water to cook in, they ran out of food), but the preschool centers were full of raggedy kids who sang for us as we looked around.

Next to one of the kitchens was a small, adobe church. Inside the church were rows of metal benches. (If I were attending services there, I would come late in order to have to stand.) The walls had been carefully whitewashed. Someone had painted a yard-high band of blue across the base of the wall behind the altar. Resting on either end of the band, as if it were a platform, were paintings of two flowerpots, all earthen colors, out of which grew golden lilies – a perfect Etruscan frieze, somehow dislocated to Lobito.

Higher up on the wall was a small sculpture of Saint Luis Gonzaga, whose name day this turned out to be. Under the close watch of a sister, four young girls were practicing a dance for the service later in the afternoon. Their feet moved in patterns almost too fast to follow as they approached the altar. Then they reached out to Saint Luis in a lovely, curving gesture and danced away again.

That afternoon, someone showed me a news dispatch saying that Angola recently bought $300 million worth of helicopter gunships and has concluded a series of agreements for support from Executive Outcomes, the mercenary service run by Afrikaners in search of new things to do. Another day in Angola with the People and the Pigs.

*   *   *

The bairros of Angola rise from the dirt, reaching across the dusty plains or up the bare hillsides on the edges of the major towns. (Every rainy season, houses are washed down the hillsides.) The houses themselves are made of dirt, which is mixed with water and dried in blocks in the intense sun. The occasional tree is grey-white with dust.

Living this way must have consequences. Years ago, in Malawi, Elena found a set of images to explain some of the differences in the spaces we and Africans inhabit. The Africans live with their bare feet in the soil, she pointed out; we plant grass and put on shoes to walk across it. On two facing pages of an album, I have pictures of this: in one photo, a sickly Malawian child sits in front of a mud hut in the dirt of his village, his skin mottled with dust and fever; in the other, four-year-old Alex stands on the lawn behind our Lilongwe house, his hands reaching out to a rainbow that is arching over the trees and flower beds. Elena felt there to be a great chasm between these two worlds, a chasm there is peril in trying to cross.

Development bureaucrats seldom try to cross the chasm. Take the preschool centers we were visiting last week. The line in WFP is that these are transformative experiences, an opportunity for children between two and five "to meet other children, learn self-discipline, and become integrated into society." (The centers are also, by coincidence, an almost effortless way for WFP to dispose of large amounts of food.) In practice, however, "self-discipline" appears to mean the ability to sit in the dirt in rows for hours at a time and to sing songs of welcome to visitors, perhaps not the most important of skills for two-year-olds. As for meeting other children and becoming integrated into society, it seems not to have occurred to anyone that these things probably happened even before the United Nations discovered Angola. The chasm between Us and Them is here so vast that *nothing* is visible on the other side.

Imagine how things must look from the African side. A group of people is living a complex, finely-tuned existence in their bairro or village, trying to make it through the day. Lovers meet, mothers nurse sick children, food gets cooked and eaten, life takes place. Suddenly, a Land Cruiser screeches to a stop in a cloud of dust. Doors burst open and out hop a clutch of smiling bureaucrats with an offer that can't be refused: do what we say, and we'll give you food, cash, tools, credit, medicine, seeds. Before you can say "community participation," the villagers are planting communal woodlots and hybrid maize, the bairro-dwellers are attending empowerment classes and sending their children to preschools. Then the bureaucrats stumble upon a New Paradigm, lose interest, and go off to something else, while the Africans try to pick up the pieces. Am I really wrong in seeing blind violence in this process?

ANGOLA

I have spent my professional life trying to understand better what is on the other side of the chasm. Everywhere I go, I poke and probe and ask endless questions – and still end up feeling I have caught only the most partial glimpses of what is there. In our boundless ignorance, how can we have the chutzpah to keep doing what we do?

The dilemma is double-edged, since an obsession with puzzling these things out wins you no friends in the bureaucracy. After last week's trip, Paul proposed that my call sign be changed from "Lima 9" to "Charlie Quebec," radio talk for "CQ" or "Chief of Questions." He was joking, but the joke had barbs.

That is the peril Elena saw in trying to cross the chasm. You never make it to the other side, but you lose your connection with your own, and tumble into the void between.

*　　　　*　　　　*

It took a while to sort out last night's events. At midnight, there was a great crash outside somewhere. Half-waking, I registered the dying away of the air conditioner and concluded that the noise was the A/C packing up as a result of a power outage. The only reasonable response was to wedge a pillow over my head and try to go back to sleep. Then the noise of people shouting at each other outside my door began to filter through the pillow. This seemed excessive as a response to a power cut. Eventually, I gave up pretending that everything was normal, and got up.

Sitting on the landing outside my flat, in a small pool of blood, was a wiry young man in his underpants. Standing over him was my guard. Neighbors came and went: one brought some clothesline and used it to tie the young man's elbows together behind him, and then to bind his feet, and then to attach the whole package to a railing. Somebody else produced handcuffs, which were pincered onto the man's wrists to the point of amputation. Another neighbor emerged from his flat with a length of rubber hose.

Then they began to beat the young man, talking conversationally with him all the while. When he began to scream or cry, they would shush him solicitously and go on with the beating. The power really had shut down (the crash had been a transformer exploding), so all this took place by flashlight, which made it difficult to register the details. I know that somebody rushed up early on with an aerosol can and sprayed something in the young man's face. The woman next door appeared later with a hypodermic needle, but the crowd of people kept me from seeing what she did with it. At one point, I realized that my guard had produced a gun from somewhere, but he didn't actually shoot the young man. Mothers brought their children to see.

I went back to bed around 2 a.m. At about the same time, there was a shoot-out in front of Silvana's house, a block up the road. Sometime in the night, the young man slipped his ropes and took off into the darkness in his underpants and handcuffs, not to be seen again. (He was lucky; in the bairros here, thieves are sometimes set on fire.) Nighttime in Luanda town.

*   *   *

This week's field trip was to Malanje to look at what is being done to help people move out of the city (to which they fled during the fighting in 1992-93) and back to their villages. I realized along the way that there are certain patterns to these trips:

Getting there gets done by plane, since so many of the roads are mined or bandit-ridden and so many of the bridges have been bombed out. WFP has its own airline for this purpose, little Caravans and Beechcraft carrying 10-12 of us. (The food aid itself gets flown around in cargo jets, mostly old Antonovs that look as if some vital part – the engines, say, or the wings – had been forgotten by the designers and pasted on after the rest of the plane had been built.) Informality is the rule: we converge on the airport at dawn, drive out to where the planes are parked, say hi to the usual pilots, strap ourselves in, and go.

I make it sound easier than it is. There are days when air traffic control feels our bribes have been insufficient, so you sit for an extra half hour on the taxiway before being cleared for takeoff. Our last flight got an even later start because the radios failed in the control tower. The pilots usually put up with all this, but not always. When we finally left Luanda on Tuesday, the Avions Sans Frontières plane just ahead of us was told by the tower to wait for an incoming jet. In no mood to cooperate, the ASF pilot gunned it out onto the runway and took off anyway. We then got a close-up view of the jet aborting its landing and struggling for altitude in order to come around for another try.

At the other end of the flight are a lot of _expatriates_, working for WFP or for the NGOs that have largely taken the place of Angola's moribund government. In Eritrea, I realized that the foreigners you meet in small African towns are mostly "saints and whiskey priests and expatriate project managers, free-lance 'journalists' and burnouts, the radically displaced." All those people are in Angola too, along with the last of the cowboys, the free spirits who love the invigorating atmosphere of a country on the edge of chaos. It strikes me that there is nothing strange about this; would you expect to find anybody _normal_ in a place like Bailundo or Malanje?

Still, it is a marvelous assortment of folks. Our base manager in Lobito is a French film director (nobody you've heard of). The guy who runs the Catholic Relief Services office in Balombo has taught English in Japan, worked on fishing boats off Alaska, and led camping tours through Mexico. The World Vision representative in Malanje is an Iowa farm boy who spent six months bicycling from Ecuador to San Diego before ending up here. (At the age of 29 or so, he is now managing a staff of 275 people, feeding thousands of demobilized soldiers in temporary quartering areas, working out evacuation plans in case the war resumes, generally taking on more responsibility than most people face in a lifetime.) The head of the UCAH office in Lobito is a Portuguese big-game hunter who used to lead safaris all over eastern and southern Africa. WFP's director of ground transport operations is an American who was born into a missionary family in Malanje and went to school there with all the Angolans who are now running the province; the family was expelled by the Portuguese shortly before independence, but he is back now running convoys around the country. Never a dull person.

The _small talk_ is rather special too. Sitting of an evening with a few beers someplace, we compare notes on local events. Cerebral malaria is going around. (A UNAVEM engineer died of it last week, and one of the expats in Malanje was evacuated for treatment in Luanda the day before I got there – she survived.) Stories of drunken soldiers with AK-47s. (A local staff member of World Vision got shot three times in the face recently when he tried to intervene in an argument between a soldier and his girlfriend.) Vehicles attacked on such-and-such stretch of road. (At least there are relatively few stories of vehicles hitting mines, mostly because everybody stays on the few cleared roads – in Angola, the road less traveled is probably mined.) Most disturbing of all, there are the stories of UNITA mortar attacks on villages, or government troop movements in violation of the ceasefire, reminders that the war could resume any time.

At the end of the evening, you retire to your _accommodation_. Take the hotel in Malanje (please!). It wasn't so much the mouse that ran across my legs in the middle of the night; it was more what I found behind the chest of drawers when I went looking for the mouse to chase it out of the room. Otherwise, the usual lack of amenities: no running water (you bathe from a bucket), no towel or soap or toilet paper (naturally, you have brought all those things with you), sporadic electricity (or none at all), insects to make a lepidopterist weep with joy (and a food aid bureaucrat just weep). I paid $8 a night for this, and thought it rather overpriced.

There are lessons to be learned even here, though. You actually _can_ take a bath in a liter of water (well, a liter and a half). It makes you realize how incredibly wasteful – at a time when Worldwatch says the world is running out of water – is the Western way of bathing: the whole of Malanje could make their morning toilet with the water from one American bathtub. Still, when I go to Windhoek next weekend, the first thing I am going to do is fill the tub with warm, bubbly water and stay there for a day.

Interspersed among all these things is the _work_ you came for. The insights come at unexpected moments: talking with a teacher and a nurse in the Cambondo resettlement area; asking the _soba_ (village chief) of Chico do Waite about his irrigation scheme; discussing road maintenance with the construction manager of the ADPP scheme in Quissala; finding out from a mother in a Lobito bairro what she thinks of the preschool center we are supporting there; looking across the bombed-out bridge over the Kuige River with the OIKOS director, trying to imagine how returnees from Malanje are going to rebuild their lives on the other side. The light breaks through at times like these, and you get one step closer to knowing what kinds of acts might be of service here.

*   *   *

Another view of whether what we do is actually of service, or whether we simply provide the palliatives that allow bad things to happen:

> I have often wondered how long the war in Angola and similar conflicts elsewhere would have continued if the United Nations and the assorted international aid agencies had not been so ready to fly in thousands of tons of food, medicine and clothes to help keep the remnants of society functioning, if they had not been there to sweep up the human rubble strewn around in the wake of battles waged in the name of the *povo* [people], if they had not provided just enough food to keep the country alive, to let the authorities avoid responsibility for their own citizens, to fatten up the young boys living in refugee camps so that they could be dragooned by one of the warring armies. The answer is probably that international aid or not, the fighting would have continued. (Karl Maier, *Angola: Promises and Lies.*)

So we stay?

*   *   *

Last week's visit to the rural areas around Malanje restored in me something I thought I had lost: my old-time love for Africa. (This had been waning in recent years, the result of too many trips to dispiriting places like Nairobi; and I thought Eritrea had killed it outright.) Like all love, the love for Africa is hard to describe, a feeling that catches you at unexpected moments somewhere between your heart and the pit of your stomach. The African light of late afternoon can call it forth, that intense glow that radiates *out* of all things, allowing you to see their innermost colors as God must always see them. A hundred other things can set loose the same feeling: the shy, bright-eyed village children; the crying of the roosters; the pride of some toothless, gummy-eyed *soba* as he shows you around his manioc garden; the half-dreamy, half-alert state of mind you achieve in your third or fourth hour of jolting across near-impassable terrain in your Land Cruiser – so many ways this can come upon you.

In Angola, the love for Africa is mixed with equal parts of pain, as you pass the WARNING: MINES signs and the destroyed villages and the amputees. (There is anger, too: *how could they do these things?*) And still... I know it tempts fate to say this, but I cannot help myself: I'm glad I'm here.

*   *   *

Yet another view of whether we should stay or go:

> Africa has to learn to help itself and is not going to until the west stops coming to the rescue. We invariably cause more problems than there were in the first place.... African countries beg for aid when they need it but it often arrives after the demand has died. Just as the country is beginning to find its feet once more, a massive excess of food arrives on the market, drives down prices and leaves farmers in need of food aid. Soon eaten, all it has done is cause more problems

and stifled growth.... The west has to accept that it has failed and allow Africa to advance at its own pace.... We have proved that we can't be trusted to meddle in Africa's affairs. To pull out will contribute more untold misery – maybe for decades – but we will no longer be interfering and adding to the problem. Until we stop propping up corrupt governments because they're better than the immediate alternative and prolonging civil wars by feeding the refugees we have helped create, there will always be blood on the tracks. (Miles Bredin, *Blood on the Tracks: A Rail Journey from Angola to Mozambique.*)

So we go?

*   *   *

This week's field trip was to Kuito. Kuito is bad, like Huambo multiplied severalfold. Most of the mines are gone from the main parts of the city, though the outskirts (and everything beyond) are still insecure. Even in the town itself, a boy blew himself apart earlier this week with a mortar shell he found in uncut grass in the central park. Driving in the countryside, we had to detour onto improvised tracks in several places because the main road is still mined. (Some people insist on using the main road anyway since it makes for faster driving, and they are gradually clearing out the anti-tank mines in the worst possible way.) You can only travel partway along the Andulo road because UNITA has mined one of the bridges as a means of discouraging you from crossing. Etc., etc.

We stayed at the house of the demining group HALO Trust. (HALO stands for Hazardous Areas Life Support Organization; it could also, say the HALO boys, stand for Half a Leg Off, har har har.) We got to watch them at work cleaning out a strip of land along a stream on the edge of town. Pretty impressive, all these guys with body armor troweling away the soil wherever their metal detectors have set up a howl. Stretchers and paramedics wait under a nearby tree. (HALO estimates that they can expect one "accident" every three months, an accident being where a deminer has a limb blown off, or worse.) They had just found a mine, which – suitably deactivated – I brought back as a souvenir. Once HALO gets done, people can start planting again, as they did before the unpleasantness of 1992-1993 left the area seeded with something more potent than onions and garlic.

The next day, 10 miles out the Chipeta road, HALO were detonating mines that were too dangerous to dig out and deactivate. These had been planted around electrical pylons to keep UNITA from taking down the power lines. UNITA had taken the lines down anyway, and the mines are now a threat only to the people who are putting in their maize crops, sometimes a yard or two from the minefields. HALO detonated four mines while we were there. It does something complicated to your stomach to watch the blast and realize that – in the absence of HALO – some of the debris would have been parts of a farmer.

The HALO people are basically your shit-kicking ex-military Brits. (They tend not to be Oxbridge graduates, and the dialogue over dinner can sound like something out of *Spinal Tap*.) Paul, their main deminer in Kuito, is a tightly wound obsessive when it comes to demining. (All the deminers seem tightly wound, perhaps no surprise.) His eyes light up when he talks about what he does, which he loves so much he says he would gladly do it for free. What he loves is The Work – he recognizes that a nice side-effect is that women and kids don't get blown apart hauling water from the stream, but that is not what gets him started in the morning.

I think, wow, in any given day Paul is probably doing more tangible good for the wretched of Kuito than I do in a year of my kind of work (or maybe in a lifetime), and he basically doesn't care. It is all wonderfully unromantic. Dom (my WFP colleague on this trip) asks about some of the South Africans who are working on demining teams in other parts of the country. A lot of those guys were first in Angola *laying* the mines; now they are back taking them out. Is part of it conscience on their part? asks Dom, and you can see Paul's brow furrow as he tries to puzzle out what Dom could possibly mean by this.

HALO itself was created in 1988 by one "Mad Mitch" (Lt.-Col. Colin Mitchell), formerly of the Argyll and Sutherland Highlanders.

Mad Mitch got his nickname in 1967, when he moved a unit of Highlanders into an area of Aden where mutineers had been killing British soldiers. Mitch chose an hour in the dead of night and marched his men into the area, bagpipers and drummers in the lead. Later he wrote, "It is the most thrilling sound in the world to go into action with the pipes playing. It stirs the blood and reminds one of the heritage of Scotland and the Regiment. Best of all, it frightens the enemy to death." The area was quickly made safe for Empire.

Mitch fell out with his commanders, though, and left the military. For a time he was a Conservative M.P., working to save the Highlanders from budget cuts, keep the U.K. out of Europe, and other worthy tasks. Then he moved on to other pursuits. The boys at HALO get a little vague in talking about just what those pursuits were, but it is known that Mitch was an adviser to Ian Smith in Rhodesia and spent time in Afghanistan during delicate periods. While in Afghanistan, he decided that demining was a job in need of doing and set up HALO. Now HALO is in places like Afghanistan, Cambodia, Mozambique and the Transcaucus as well as Angola, taking out mines (and, almost incidentally, keeping women and kids from being dismembered). Go figure.

We also traveled around visiting WFP projects having to do with resettlement, road repair, agriculture, preschool centers, stuff like that. It is the demining that lingers in the mind, though.

*   *   *

I haven't known quite how to record the bedlam in the midst of which I live here at my apartment, but I suppose I should try. (My Portuguese dictionary translates "bedlam" as "manicómio," and then translates "manicómio" as "lunatic asylum," which at least conveys something of the flavor of the place.) One problem is that I cannot figure out exactly what creates some of the noises that make up the bedlam. I've tried, though, and here is my best guess as to what is going on:

There is The Fool in the apartment above mine. He stepped on a mine somewhere during the War and blew his legs off and lost his mind. Even though he sits on his stumps on the floor, they are afraid he might oonch his way out the door, so they have tied him to a chair leg. To keep him entertained, they give him a couple of marbles, which he tosses in the air and lets roll across the floor. TAP TAPTAP TAPPITTY TAPPITTY RRRRRLLLLL. Then he drags himself across the floor, taking the chair with him. SCRRRRCCHHHHH. Then he repeats the process: TAP TAPTAP TAPPITTY TAPPITTY RRRRRLLLL SCRRRRCCHHHHH. In losing his mind, he acquired X-ray vision, so he always knows where I am and drags his chair to the room above in order to roll his marbles there. He also lost his need for sleep, so this goes on all day, all evening, at 1:00 a.m., 2:00 a.m.... On Saturday and Sunday mornings, early, they give him a hammer to play with, and he pounds it on the floor for several hours: BANG BANG BANG BANG BANG BANG BANG BANG.

Then there are the Madwomen of Maianga, who roam the streets all day howling mournfully at passers-by: kakakakaka OOOOOEEEEEEEEEE kakakakaka OOOOOEEEEEEEEE.

Meanwhile, the traffic rages outside, night and day, a mixture of cars (RRRRRRR, WHOOOOOSHH) and trucks (RMMMMMM) and motorcycles (PUTTA PUTTA PUTTA KIKIKIKIKIKI ZZZZZZNNNNNNNG). Along with this comes what everyone calls the "Angolan doorbell," the endless line of drivers parked in front of the building blowing their horns in hopes their friends will eventually notice and come down to say hello. (BEEP BEEP BEEPBEEPBEEP BEEEEEEEEP.) The Angolan doorbell starts getting rung around 6:30 a.m. and goes on more or less nonstop until midnight, though I have heard it as late as 4:00 in the morning and as early as 5:00.

At appointed times, someone assembles a couple of dozen children on the landing outside my door. Specially recruited for their extreme hyperactivity and lung power, the children have trained by watching videos of University of Miami football games, so they can all scream incomprehensibly at once, clapping rhythmically at the same time. (CLAP CLAP CLAP CLAP EEEEEEK YAAAAAHHHH OOOOOOOOHH.) Their assigned hours for doing this are 6-10 p.m. weekdays and the couple of hours after lunch on Saturday and Sunday afternoons.

One of Angola's most prominent inventors used to live across the street. One day, he was testing a new kind of car alarm, designed to immobilize potential thieves by making them crazy with the noise. When he turned it on, it made *him* crazy, and he had to be taken away. Nobody knows how to turn the thing off, though (he had ensured it couldn't be deactivated without a code only he knows), so the alarm has set itself off several times every hour since: EEEEEEaaaaaa EEEEEEaaaaa WIP WIP WIP WIP WIP ooooEEEEEE ooooEEEEEE WIP WIP WIP WIP WIP.

A couple of floors above me lives an electrical engineer who runs his sound amplification system through a continuous testing process on days when it is not on loan for major rock shows. To give the system a fair test, he uses it for the world's most awful music, the bass lines of which filter through the thickest floors and the most potent earplugs: CHUNKA CHUNKA CHUNKA CHUNKA TADUMP TADUMP TADUMP TADUMP CHUNKA CHUNKA CHUNKA CHUNKA. (I wonder sometimes whether turning his amplifier up to 11 would bring the whole building down around us; as it is, you can feel the pulsations in the soles of your feet, or leaning on your balcony railing, or touching the walls.) He has cousins in every building within earshot, and they have systems of their own which they test with music that is even worse than his.

It goes without saying that from every direction there are also the dogs: RUF RUF RUF RUF RUF GRRRRR GRRRRRR SNARLL SNAP YIPYIPYIPYIPYIPYIP RUF RUF RUF RUF.

Those are just the constant noises. As an occasional leaven, there is also the statue of the Miraculous Virgin in the garden of the house next to our building. When the mood is upon her, the Virgin shouts insults at the young men of the neighborhood, and they congregate in great crowds to shout back, and to shout at each other, and to get into fights, until the proprietors of the Virgin come out and throw buckets of water on them through the gates of the house. (YAYAYAYAYAYYAYAY HEY HEY HEY THUNK SPLAAASSSSH AIIEEEEEE.)

I may have missed the odd detail as to who is actually making these noises, and why. I'll bet I'm not far off, though. The point is, *the noises and events are there exactly as I describe them*, which means that when I return home after a field trip or a tough day at the office, I am immersed in this:

TAP TAPTAP TAPPITTY TAPPITTY RRRRRLLLL SCRRRRCCHHHHH RUF RUF RUF RUF RUF GRRRRR GRRRRRR SNARLL SNAP YIPYIPYIPYIPYIPYIP RUF RUF RUF RUF RMMMMMM EEEEEEaaaaaa EEEEEEaaaaa WIP WIP WIP WIP WIP ooooEEEEEE ooooEEEEEE WIP WIP WIP WIP WIP RRRRRRR WHOOOOOSHH CLAP CLAP CLAP CLAP EEEEEEK YAAAAAHHHH OOOOOOOHH CHUNKA CHUNKA CHUNKA CHUNKA TADUMP TADUMP TADUMP TADUMP CHUNKA CHUNKA CHUNKA CHUNKA PUTTA PUTTA PUTTA KIKIKIKIKIKI ZZZZZZNNNNNNNG BANG BANG BANG BANG BANG BANG BANG BANG kakakakaka OOOOOEEEEEEEEEE kakakakaka OOOOOEEEEEEEEEE BEEP BEEP BEEPBEEPBEEP BEEEEEEEEP YAYAYAYAYAYYAYAY HEY HEY HEY THUNK SPLAAASSSSH AIIEEEEEE CLAP CLAP CLAP CLAP EEEEEEK YAAAAAHHHH OOOOOOOHH...

For somebody as hypersensitive to noise as I am, this is heavy stuff, and I am not at all sure I am going to make it out of here with my mind intact. The possibility of being blown apart by mines or bandits is *nothing* compared with this. The people who say that God never asks of you more than you can take never lived in a Luandan apartment.

*   *   *

Meanwhile, out in the Real World, the "Peace Process" follows its own lack of momentum. UNITA ended their party congress in Bailundo last week, and their radio then reported they would meet none of their current obligations under the Lusaka Protocols: the generals would not come to Luanda to join the federal army, Savimbi would not accept a vice-presidency, nothing further would happen until the constitution was rewritten and the electoral process over-hauled in order to be less "biased" (as it was in 1992, apparently, when Savimbi lost the elections).

I would have viewed this as bad news, but the U.N. politicos here say everything is fine; what seems bad news is just UNITA establishing a bargaining position for the talks Savimbi is shortly to have with President dos Santos. I had thought they had already had their "talks," in order to come up with the Lusaka Protocols and that the job was now to implement the Protocols; but life is apparently more complex than that.

Or so it can appear, at least, at senior levels of the United Nations in Luanda. The United Nations feels responsible for the peace, and therefore there is peace, and will be peace. It sounds like descriptions of the events of 1992, when the outside mediators talked all year about the democratic elections they were supervising and the triumphs of national reconciliation and – gosh, excuse me for a second if radio contact is interrupted as I head for my bunker, but all is very well – and were still babbling bromides as they were dragged onto their evacuation flights with the Battle of Luanda raging around them.

The most embarrassing of the current self-delusions has to do with "demobilization." The pivot of the peace process is the disposition of the UNITA army, 60,000 troops now in the "quartering areas" from which they will be integrated into the federal army or demobilized. No more UNITA army, no more war. Luanda has an entire industry (including much of WFP's senior staff) in constant meetings to arrange the logistics of the quartering areas, to feed the soldiers, see that they are retrained and reintegrated into society, coddled and cared for. The whole operation has been so successful that large numbers of the quartering areas are now officially "closed," while the details are worked out of how to send the soldiers there home.

Only one problem – *what soldiers?* If you visit an actual quartering area in an actual place (as I did in Malanje), the expats on the ground make no pretense that there are any soldiers there. When the U.N. began to put the heat on Savimbi to get the demobilization underway, his people simply rounded up anyone they found in the villages at hand, told them they were "soldiers," gave them the equivalent of cardboard weapons, and sent them off to the camps. Desperate to be seen to have made peace, the U.N. counted the cardboard weapons and the old men and the farmers and young boys and declared the quotas met. Meanwhile, as everyone but senior U.N. staffers are aware, Savimbi's actual army works out in its bases across the border in Zaire and prepares for whatever is coming.

It is classic U.N.-think: the U.N. is responsible for the peace, so there is peace, so there are soldiers where there are none and none where there are. To see the UNITA soldiers in Zaire instead of in the quartering areas is to be disloyal to the peace and to the United Nations. Loyalty means seeing what *should* be going on. It is perfectly straightforward, if you have worked long enough for the United Nations. All is very well, and – what? what? I only read your radio transmission two by five here in my bunker, what's that about an evacuation flight?

The deck is badly stacked. If, miraculously, peace should prevail in spite of the fantasizers, they will take full credit. If things do go wrong, this will be blamed on the people who saw the soldiers in Zaire. Never underestimate the advantage of being able to establish the terms of the dialogue.

* * *

I have been rereading Dag Hammarskjöld's *Markings*, one of my most treasured books. Given the unreality of the discussions about the peace process, I circulated around the office the following "Marking":

> Respect for the word is the first commandment in the discipline by which a man can be educated to maturity – intellectual, emotional and moral. Respect for the word – to employ it with scrupulous care and an incorruptible heart-felt love of truth – is essential if there is to be any growth in a society or in the human race. To misuse the word is to show contempt for man. It undermines the bridges and poisons the wells. It causes man to regress down the long path of his evolution.

I wanted to show that there was once a time when even a U.N. Secretary-General could talk about things like "respect for the word." Our newest arrival, a young British woman here to work on public relations, emailed back: "David, good stuff, but it does seem life-times away!!"

It is really hard to keep going sometimes...

*　　　　　*　　　　　*

It's not just English; I'm having the odd problem with Portuguese as well. I'm struggling to gain some minimal competence in the language in order to communicate with the folks around me. I keep running into words, though, that it's hard to imagine dropping unobtrusively into conversation:

aprosopia (s.f.) -- the quality of having no face
inculcadeira (s.f.) -- woman who practices inculculation
testicondo (adj.) -- said of the horse whose testicles are not in sight

*　　　　　*　　　　　*

Senhora Palmira is always impressed at the degree of environmental bedlam when she comes over to give me my Portuguese lessons. As a Portuguese-Angolan, she blames it on the *Angolan*-Angolans, or, as she refers to them, "selvagens" (savages). Last week when she came, the engineer and his cousins were all testing their sound systems at once. Senhora Palmira stood there amazed. "This is not even Angolan," she finally said; "this is Congolese."

My job is to use this for my practice. I need to learn to stop resisting the noises, to stop wanting them not to be there. Stephen Levine talks about learning to keep your heart open in hell; you should be able to remain open-hearted in a Luandan apartment.

I remember once, stoned at a campsite in the Virgin Islands, discovering how to take the night sounds, one by one, and bring them inside myself: the water, the crickets, the wind. Eventually, there was nothing left outside. I had become without boundaries, all-encompassing, all-accepting. It was easy to do with sounds like those; what is necessary is to do the same with the sounds of Luanda: the Angolan doorbell, the screaming children, The Fool upstairs, the car alarms. What a lesson it would be, to learn to be all-accepting of things like these.

I have come upon a powerful tool for this particular practice: walking meditation. I don't think I could do anything as subtle as sitting meditation in the midst of the bedlam, but walking gives you stronger things to meditate upon. You realize that no matter how great the chaos around you, you can still feel your feet planting themselves, carrying you along, lifting off the floor and swinging forward again. If you can be attentive to something that fundamental in the midst of the noise, what is there to fear?

*　　　　*　　　　*

Violent crime has fallen in New York City. The former police commissioner attributes this to the fact that he began to prosecute small crimes as well as large ones. When people started getting arrested for littering and jaywalking, the murder rate dropped. This makes a certain intuitive sense – if there is insistence that the routine moments of life embody mutual respect rather than disrespect, people simply have to go further to arrive at an act of major violence.

I reflect on this as I experience the constant bedlam here. People think nothing of invading each other's spaces with noise, and little of having their own space invaded. This turns easily into invasion with objects: the walkway in front of my apartment fills constantly with papers and bones and banana peels, as people on the floors above miss the gaps in the landing in tossing garbage out their doors. This turns into invasion with fists, and then with knives, and then with guns. To make the "Peace Process" work, perhaps what Angola really needs are Noise Police.

ANGOLA

*   *   *

Savimbi remains intransigent about the "Peace Process" and is holed up in his bunker, refusing to talk with anyone. The boys at HALO have had to pull out of northern Bie Province altogether because UNITA has started to re-mine roads that had previously been cleared. All is well, all is well, all is very well...

*   *   *

The electricity has been crashing for the last couple of weeks, giving me the chance to make lots of command decisions about whether the stuff in the freezer can be cooked at once or must simply be tossed out. Then the power came back for the rest of the neighborhood but stayed off for three days in my apartment and the one next door. For half a day of this I had running water anyway because the city supply was on and I didn't need the pump; the rest of the time I dipped water from a trash can into the Super Camp Shower I bought in Dublin and bathed in the drip. The man next door told me that he didn't care, he could always tap into the power supply of the neighbor on the other side, so if I wanted it fixed I could fix it myself. You have to find your own *electricista* in a case like this – people just smile when you suggest it is the electricity company's job to provide electricity – so I finally arranged that this morning. Then I turned on the pump to get some water from the tank, only to find the tank bone-dry: my five-day reserve of water had somehow evaporated over a two-day period when I couldn't tap into it because the power was off.

Where did the water go? Somewhere, and it is still going. My colleague and friend Nick Tremblin arranged to have a truckload of water pumped in this afternoon, and my tape measure shows the new water slowly draining away. The pump, which works only when you open a tap, turns itself on every thirty seconds or so when all the taps are off, dutifully pumping water – where? By tomorrow the tank will be dry again, so I have washed my underwear and the dishes and myself, flushed the toilet, filled up my trash can, and will try to figure out in the morning what to do next.

I know that all moments are equal: writing a poem, washing out my underwear in a fleeting moment when the water is on, making love (not that that is an option just now), finding a candle to open a tin of soup for dinner, drawing a flower, tossing my garbage into the pile outside (more than a yard deep today and thirty or forty feet down the whole of one lane of the street), doing walking meditations, cleaning up the mess where the sewer gas has blown all the water out of the toilet... It is a great blessing to be able to experience all these equal moments, I'm sure.

*　　　*　　　*

It has been a long weekend. I had two people working on the water system from 8 yesterday morning until 2, including a trip to the Praça de Golf (a vast outdoor market – out past the airport, turn left, and keep going) to look for a cutoff valve when the original one had its threads stripped in trying to insert a one-way valve a half inch bigger than the old one into a maze of pipes with no play at all, and then when Nick went home and I had delivered Benvindo, the Angolan plumber, to his house, the power went on for the first time all day so I was able to turn on the pump, which exposed the leaks downstream of the one-way valve that they hadn't been able to diagnose in the absence of water, meaning that I then had to go get the plumber again and let him work fixing the leaks until about 4, at which time I came to the office for a long meeting with the bridge-demining mission.

Then this morning, the city water went on for the first time for several days, and the pipes *up*stream of the one-way valve (through which the water pumped out of the reserve tank doesn't run, at least when the one-way valve is working, and which therefore leaks only when there is city water) began to leak and I had to go out again to get the plumber, who worked for a while, turning one leak into four (the miracle of the loaves and leaks), at which point he decided that only *cola de metal* (metal glue) would do, requiring a tour of three Luandan open markets, ending up at the Praça de Golf (out past the airport, turn left, and go waaay out there), none of which had *cola de metal*, so we came back and the leaks had mostly healed themselves and we decided to take a break from it all and by then it was 1:30 and I washed the clothes and hung them out and had lunch and now I'm here at the office.

Sandwiched in between the two days was a looong night of boozing and bonding with the boys: Paul Buffard (the guy I had tried to take as my deputy to Eritrea, but who was on the Executive Director's shitlist at the time so they turned him down and tried to fire him, but who somehow managed to survive and ended up here), and Nick (who was in Eritrea doing a job for us when I was tossed out last year and who then floated for a while and finally came to rest in Angola), and some disheveled Swede, and me. We sat in an outdoor Angolan bar on some dark back street for longer than I can remember and drank more beers than I can remember, and I guess I somehow drove home because that's where I woke up this morning at 7:00 when the city water went on and I started dealing with the leaks.

It was a bit of intense, and a lot of various. Today's comparative market-going was something I hadn't done much of here before, and I give the whole exercise two stars (worth the detour). You can buy *anything* in an open Luandan market (toilet seats, nails, boom boxes, fresh shrimp, cigarettes, toothpaste, metal chains, Coca-Cola, dolls, shut-off valves, cap pistols, salami sandwiches, fuses, light bulbs, Lycra panties, buckets) – well, everything except *cola de metal*. At the market in the equivocal part of town (relative even to mine, for example, which means *equivocal*), we had to buy our way out of a small mob of hostile kids who were threatening to rip the mirrors off the car unless we gave them money. (Beggary has no boundaries here: I was walking out of my place yesterday afternoon, and a schoolgirl, headed into the building with her bookbag, asked me for dinheiro as we passed each other on the stairs.) The place way out of town, on the other hand, was a lot more laid back, nobody hassling you to watch your car, lines of women resting in the dirt by their identical piles of goods (in the section where we were looking, that meant a couple of tubes of silicone adhesive, a tray of nails, and a roll of electrical tape), the sun shimmering over what must have been 50 acres of baked market.

Going to collect Benvindo this morning, I ended up sitting in a plastic chair outside his place while he went off with a bucket to bathe and get dressed. It was your basic urban, baked-earthblock house, a couple of dogs outside licking and biting at their scabs and sores, kids running around in rags, a stream of unbelievably filthy sewage running nearby, from which women were hauling buckets of water home. In the dirt outside Benvindo's door were two carefully-tended pots of flowers. A little girl broke off a flower, crept up behind a friend, stuck the flower in her hair, and then chased her around the house laughing until the flower fell out. Sunday in Luanda town.

I found last night strangely moving. You get such a curious assortment of expatriates in a place like this, the kind of people you really need Graham Greene or William Boyd to describe. There are a lot of cowboys who chased the emergency here and who patch together some kind of day work in order to do the nighttime disco circuit with their beautiful, incredibly bored-looking Angolan girlfriends, and kind of linger on and on in shadow. The disheveled Swede was one of those (though last night without his girlfriend). These people are not without interest or the unexpected quirk: one of my later memories of the evening was the Swede going off on a long improvisation on ideas from Hesse's *Siddhartha*.

It is Nick and Paul who tear at me, though. Who knows what steps have gotten them finally here, but they lead the kinds of lives that from the outside you would describe as desperate: without creature comforts, without professional acknowledgement, without job security, and without their families. They try to keep in touch – Paul had a $1,000 phone bill last month – but the kids grow up scanning their birthday cards to Papa into digital format and sending them off by email. Nick's kids are seven and nine, and he has just bought the family a house in Swindon, which he will hardly set foot in. They were with him during an earlier job in Angola (UNITA swept through their town once during the war, and Nick had to establish a defensive position with an AK-47, while his family huddled in the bathtub), but it wouldn't work now. He is completely uncomplaining (as is Paul), but after the sixth or seventh beer on a Saturday night, he turns to me and says, "David, sometimes it is so hard," and his face is full of pain.

A weekend of odd angles and glints of light. I have no idea what to make of it.

ANGOLA

*   *   *

I spent two hours yesterday driving a ten-year-old with a bullet in his stomach around Luanda, trying to find a hospital that would care for him. The bullet had entered at the lower left side of his abdomen and stayed near the surface – you could feel it down below his navel – so nothing vital was shattered or hemorrhaging. This was lucky for the ten-year-old, since every hospital we went to turned him away: no emergency service, not responsible, not interested, please don't block the driveway. We finally ended up at a private clinic, where they agreed to deal with the bullet if I paid the bills. I'll find out tomorrow what happened next.

The boy had gotten in the way of somebody's attempt to hijack sacks of grain from a truck driving away from the port. The guards opened fire, and the ten-year-old was the one who got shot. (We are talking downtown Luanda here.) When I happened by a couple of minutes later, a mob of people blocked my car, two guys piled in with the kid, and off we went.

I never did figure out the relationship between the guys and the kid, but they seemed genuinely concerned about getting care for him; at one point, when it became clear that public hospitals had little interest in us, they stopped me, darted off into a nearby slum, and reappeared with perhaps $4 they had assembled to pay for the boy's treatment. (Touching, but not the price of private surgery, even in Luanda.) Later, though, when we chanced to cross paths with an Angolan colleague of mine from WFP, she took one look at them, labeled them "bandits," and made me promise not to drive them home at the end of our adventure for fear of losing car or life. I had thought about these possibilities (we Luandans are wary souls) but had decided their interest was in the boy. Who knows, who knows.

The image that lingers is of a boy with a gunshot wound and absolutely nowhere to go with it. Something terrible has happened to this place, and there is no way to imagine setting it right.

*　　　　*　　　　*

Should we be working in places like Angola or not (cont.)? Here is a perspective from William D. Montalbano, a *Los Angeles Times* staff writer, in an article published today on humanitarian aid in places like Chechnya, Rwanda, Somalia, etc. ("Is Giving Aid Worth the Risk?"):

> The glum new reality is that humanitarian aid, impelled by the moral imperative to help the needy, may – tragically – do more harm than good in lawless lands.... In Liberia, every rebel offensive in the last four years has been preceded by systematic lootings of aid organizations. More than 400 vehicles and millions of dollars in supplies have been stolen at gunpoint to feed and supply gunmen or to be sold in the markets of neighboring countries.... "A Liberian warlord said to me one day, 'I can starve a village until the children die, and then you will come with food and medicine which I will take, and no one can do anything about it,'" recalled American aid worker Martha Carey. He was right, said Carey, who was stunned to find one village in which children had starved, families had been massacred, and survivors begged: "Don't bring food, don't bring anything, it makes things worse. Just go and leave us alone."

So we go?

*　　　　*　　　　*

We were on a beach yesterday an hour's drive south of Luanda. In mid-afternoon, there was the rumble of an explosion from the general direction of the city, and then we could see dense smoke rising. More explosions followed, more columns of smoke. At one point, there was an enormous fireball, and a mushroom cloud rising thousands of feet into the air above it. A couple of minutes later (we were at least 20 miles away), we heard the blast. Then more explosions and smoke. The whole thing went on for perhaps ninety minutes. The WFP radio system was passing urgent messages back and forth: the explosion was in a munitions dump on the eastern edge of town, our warehouse on that side was badly damaged, the airport was functioning normally, stuff like that. Luanda radio eventually reported that everything was under control (while we watched the explosions continue), then said a communiqué would be issued later. No communiqué has yet been issued.

When we got back to the city later, it was as if nothing had happened. We stopped by the Rialto for a dinner of beer and prawns, and the only problem was getting a table. My driver laughed and laughed on the way to the office this morning, describing how everyone in his bairro had thought the war had broken out again and had been running away. That hadn't lasted long, apparently, and people in other parts of town barely reacted. Luanda radio did say there had been no casualties, and everybody seems willing (or anxious) to believe that and go on about their day.

The Portuguese word used locally at times like this is that everything is "*normal*" (with the accent on the second syllable), and I suppose it is, for Luanda. The prevailing reaction to yesterday is basically that nothing happened; and if it did, it didn't mean anything; and if it meant anything, it is over now. This is flatly incredible, given what we were seeing from twenty miles away, but a strange state of mind prevails here, involving a lot of heavy denial.

The denial mentality affects expatriates as well as Angolans, and my colleagues here are treating the matter pretty lightly this morning (including one woman living several miles away who was nearly knocked off her feet by the main blast). I have noticed this before: when one of our staff, or an expatriate somewhere, is killed, office gossip immediately has the victim involved with the Governor's mistress, or in something illicit to do with diamonds, whatever might mean that the rest of us (who don't consort with mistresses or diamonds) are exempt. Yesterday is over, and it won't happen again; how about a beer?

The world these days must be full of people like us, living in the here and now, numbed to things going on beyond their periphery.

You can understand the reasons we have to protect ourselves, but isn't something wrong here?

*   *   *

I have been thinking about what it does to my perspective on Africa to have been working here on and off for 36 years, in contrast to the ways relative newcomers see things. This has come up in talking with Howard Standen, a Brit who arrived here two weeks ago to set up our Vulnerability Analysis and Mapping Unit. Howard was born a couple of years after I first touched down in Addis Ababa in 1961. He became conscious of Africa during Zimbabwe's war of independence and has spent a lot of time in Southern Africa since.

What Howard mostly knows, though, is the Africa of the past 15 years. What he knows nothing of (except by hearsay and reading history books) is the way Africa felt in that 1960s period of continental liberation. For me, there were at least two memorable aspects of that time: the way things were put together then, the colonial interspersed among the traditional; and the sense everywhere of political optimism and hope.

I thought about the way things used to be while driving back from the beach last weekend. We drove through countryside that once would have been scattered with villages of simple, thatched-roof houses, surrounded by fields of maize. People would have been plowing or harvesting, hauling water and firewood, pretty much the way they had been doing these things for centuries. Every fifty miles would be a provincial center, simple low buildings for the traders and administrators, the main street clean and quiet.

Now the villages are gone, razed for plantations (themselves long gone now) or cleared out by mines. Rusting vehicles are scattered by the roadside, along with piles of discarded plastics, tin cans, bones. At one point, someone has tried to build a golf course, all packed earth and scrub brush. (A healthy drive would bounce and roll forever.) Slums line the roads for miles outside town, shacks with rusted roofs, young men with fading T-shirts and urban swagger and no prospects.

The places where administrators and traders did their business are a study in decay, walls cracked and only the memory of paint.

I don't want to romanticize the old Africa – it was a tough life, which everyone with a choice has moved beyond. Still, it had a completeness and dignity and sense of order to it that no longer exist, and these are not things to minimize. Angola has not moved from the traditional to the modern; it has lost the traditional and let whatever was once modern collapse. It makes me think of a wonderful quote from Antonio Gramsci: "The old is dying and the new cannot be born; in this interregnum a great variety of morbid symptoms appear."

Howard doesn't remember Africa this way. As we drove back from the beach last weekend, he kept looking with delight at the ocean beyond piles of garbage he hardly noticed; I loved seeing the ocean too, but felt constantly jarred by the garbage and the wrecked vehicles and rusting roofs and urban swaggerers. The old world described by writers such as Laurens van der Post, a world I at least caught glimpses of long ago, is for Howard history or archeology, not something to mourn. I feel great pangs of compassion for him, for all he never saw, and a rush of gratefulness that I was there to see it before it was gone.

Howard also knows nothing of the sense of idealism that swept across Africa in the early 1960s. The Mboyas and Kenyattas and Nyereres and Kaundas of the time spoke so eloquently about freedom and justice and hope. In a cynical age, it is difficult to believe any more that they actually meant it; but I believe they did, at least at first. It was a wonderful time to be young and in Africa, and I seem to have made then a life commitment to the place.

For his part, all Howard has ever known is the Africa of Moi and Mobutu, where every government has collapsed into corruption and decay, and half of every population is in bloody war with the other half. Howard takes this for granted, as a field on which to map and analyze vulnerability. What can it be like to make a commitment to such a place?

Africa has become a violent slum on a continental scale, and there seems to be no bottom to the slide. I look at Howard and realize how much easier it is never to have known Africa's special wonder or its hopes. I do not envy him that ignorance at all; but I am so sad.

*   *   *

Morning. Janse Sorman and I have a brief exchange on the way to our offices:

J: *"Tudo bom?"*
D: *"Nao."*
J: *"Tudo mau?"*
D: *"Si."*
J: *"É normal."*

(J: "All well?"
D: "No."
J: "All bad?"
D: "Yes."
J: "It's normal.")

*   *   *

I was driving to work a few days ago, and there was suddenly an egret-tree where none had been before, maybe 30 snow-white egrets scattered through the branches of a sickly tree clinging to life in piles of garbage down by the Maianga roundabout. I felt the way someone in prison must feel when a lizard runs unexpectedly across the wall of his cell – something to look at other than bars. They were so beautiful.

*   *   *

Driving back to the office from UNDP yesterday morning, we came around the corner by the Presidente Hotel and found a mob of people on both sides of the street, very soberly watching a young man who was lying in the road, his trouser leg soaked in blood. He had tried to steal something, and a policeman had shot him. There were police around, but nobody seemed to be doing much about him. We drove the remaining fifty yards to the office, and the next time I looked out the street had cleared.

After work, I was home having my Portuguese lesson when there were three shots in an apartment in one of the floors above mine. My teacher and I went out the door to look – everybody in the building was out by then, looking up toward where the shots must have come from, talking back and forth, not very concerned. Eventually we all went back inside again. My teacher shrugged and smiled and went on with the lesson.

I'm not fully acclimatized, I guess; I find it hard to relax here.

*   *   *

I've just been reading the U.N. Resident Coordinator's last quarterly report on the security situation in Angola. The report's basic conclusions are more or less what you would expect: "The general security situation remains volatile. Policemen are unpredictable. [Actually, they are all too predictable; see below.] Criminal activities such as highway banditry, robbery perpetrated by common bandits and deserted soldiers have been reported. Violent and fatal armed attack occurred against UN staff. Detention, intimidation and harassment to UN Agency personnel have been reported. Crimes are becoming more frequent and more violent in Luanda. A new pattern of crime has emerged which involves expatriates being targeted at the airport based on their suitcases and attacked on their way into town in a professional, tactical manner." Etc. etc.

What I like, though, are some of the details, which often imply (but never quite tell) wonderful stories:

> - Luanda. The NGO called CMDA lost a Toyota Hilux in downtown Luanda to an armed carjacking. Due to an alert Guard Force member, the vehicle was spotted being loaded onto a large cargo plane for transport to another part of the country. The thieves were caught and turned out to be local police.

- During the holidays, any citizen caught shooting randomly on the street was shipped off to a prison in the Namib desert. They are now being brought back to the city for trial. [The holidays over, it's okay to shoot randomly on the street again?]

- Luanda, Kinaxixe Area, around 02:00 hours on 03 November. An armed and police uniformed group stopped a UNDP staff member for search. They stole his portable Motorola radio and cash $300.

- Luanda, Kinaxixe Area, around 03:00 hours on 03 November. An armed and police uniformed group stopped a UNDP staff member. They searched him in person and fortunately they could not find anything to steal. [That's because they had taken it all at 02:00 hours.]

- Luanda. An Australian citizen with a South African passport, currently working for Saracen Demining, was attacked while driving his car near the Texaco offices. Eight commandos forced his car to a stop and stabbed the man in the leg with a bayonet as he attempted to escape. For some unknown reason [?!], the man was carrying 130,000 US dollars in his vehicle and when the commandos saw the money, their attention turned away allowing him to escape.

- Luanda. A security meeting participant stated that he arrived at the Luanda airport, picked up his luggage and was waiting to exit the customs check when someone grabbed his suitcase and ran out. The officials kept him in line and would not let him pursue the thief.

- [And perhaps most mysterious of all:] Luanda. Parts of a UNDP staff member were stolen close to the building by unknown robbers.

What do you suppose it means when you start getting used to all this?

ANGOLA

*   *   *

We flew back from Uige on Thursday through a sky like no other I have seen. The pilots were improvising a path through a line of storms – I watched with them as the radar presented great, shifting clots of menace through which our suddenly-fragile little propeller plane had to thread its way. Out the window were banks of clouds towering to the top of the sky, then sudden views into a pastel infinity (an artist's rendering of the atmosphere of some exotic planet), then lightless, dimensionless grays closing around us like death itself, then the shimmer of a curling river far below reflecting the slanting sun of late afternoon, then another glimpse outward to some far place exempt from the usual rules of perspective or up and down. When we landed in Luanda, the captain – a young South African I hadn't flown with before – said, "It makes you realize how small you are," and I could only agree.

That wasn't the most intimate glimpse we got into mortality this trip. My colleague Mercedes took me to visit the clinic we support in Uige for people with long, wasting diseases like sleeping sickness and tuberculosis. There was a mother there with a memorable face, all strength and humor and bright intelligence, someone you would want to settle in with for a long talk about real things. That day, though, the most real thing for her was her child, a three-year-old who had gotten sleeping sickness and then tuberculosis and who was clearly dying. We shared alarm for a moment over the state of the child's teeth, which were all brown and crusty and ready to crumble away, but that was mostly a way of denying what was happening to the rest of the child – when Mercedes passed her hand in front of its vacant eyes, there was no response. I wanted to go back the next day to see what had become of it, but didn't have the nerve.

There were positive moments, too, as we talked with the Government and UNITA agriculture people about things we might all do to promote food security in the province. Any of these things would depend on a stable peace, though, and the prospects for this remain uncertain. We visited a quartering area where UNITA troops are supposed to be staying pending demobilization and the creation of a government of national unity. It turns out, though, that the "troops" are actually the underaged and infirm of the area, herded by UNITA into the camp to fulfill its quotas. The actual UNITA troops remain at large, where they get food diverted from the rations provided for fictitious "dependents" of the fictitious "troops" in the camps. The "peace process" then records "demobilization," while units of the UNITA army remain intact and well fed – with intent to do what?

The Government is not unmindful of the situation. While we were in Uige, there was a state of heightened security, barricades in front of the Governor's office and troop movements at night. According to the peace agreements, Uige is one of the provinces which is to shift to a UNITA administration when the government of national unity is implemented; but I wouldn't count on this happening soon, or without a fight.

The people who control events are a little scary. Uige's governor happened to be in town last week (he prefers Luanda), and he granted us an audience. He is an imposing man – built somewhat like an upright freezer – who arrived (70 minutes after our appointed time) with his undershirt showing from underneath a short-sleeved military tunic. He wore a very thin, very gold watch and a gold ring that served as the setting for a double row of diamonds. All bristles, he lectured us for our effrontery in suggesting that our project would be carried out in both "Government" and "UNITA" zones – there is only one Government in Uige, he informed us, of which he is the governor. (We refrained from asking him when he was last in Negage, the UNITA provincial capital we were to visit the following day.) Then he graciously arranged a meeting for us with his technical staff and swept out into the night. According to his business card, the governor's name is Serafim.

When we arrived in Negage, we got an offsetting set of lectures from the UNITA officials. In their case, they wanted to make clear that it would be unacceptable to have NGOs implement our project. This discomfited the NGO members of our mission, who had been told they were there to implement the project, and we left in some confusion. Perhaps UNITA has more important things to think about.

In the face of what might come, people do what they do: the doctors treat the sick in the clinic, the agriculturists work on ways to help the displaced become farmers again, the farmers harvest their crops, the mother comforts her dying child. Everybody hopes that whoever is running things finds a safe path between the storms, but we are talking about people with an apparent compulsion to steer straight for the thunderheads.

Pray for Uige.

*   *   *

I never know what is going on here. I was sitting in front of the fan last night, trying to keep cool, when there was a shot outside. Standing ankle-deep in the pile of garbage across the street was a man waving a gun. People were ducking behind cars, but with no particular sense of urgency. Kids arrived from various directions to watch, keeping a respectful distance.

The man walked into the street. Then someone I hadn't noticed before got up slowly from where he had been lying in the garbage. I supposed he had been shot, but he was moving okay. A car accelerated out of a side street, then screeched to a stop in the middle of the road, and the man with the gun jumped into it. The second man ran in front of the car and began to shout and point at it. As the car accelerated, he dived for the curb. The car missed him, disappearing around the corner. Still shouting, the man ran after it, followed by perhaps fifty spectators. When they didn't reappear, I went back to my fan.

What could it have been all about?

*   *   *

The place is terminally getting to me – I feel like I'm going down for the last time. I ended up sleeping on the floor in the front room last night because the screaming children and the pounding blare of the upstairs neighbor's "music" on the bedroom side was too much to handle, even with earplugs and air conditioner and pillow over the head. When I got up in the middle of the night to move back (the front room doesn't work in the early mornings, when the people line up in their cars outside the building to blow their horns at their friends), the air conditioner smelled of smoke and was clearly about to melt down. The power was off this morning, water only comes two hours at a time now, perhaps three days a week, job satisfaction is zero as usual. *É normal*, but I can't take much more of it. The upcoming Easter weekend has me in a state of the most terrible dread – *four days in that place???!*

"God is the maker of heaven and earth, of all that is seen and unseen." I listen to the gunshots and the brutal, ugly noise; I think of the Angolans for whom all this is the only, inescapable reality (at least I have a hope of escaping someday); I try to imagine God making this; and I get very confused.

I was in the midst of my walking meditation on Sunday when the neighbor's music kicked in. Okay, I thought, I will take on the heart of God and view this without judgment, with detachment, with merciful awareness. So I did that for a few minutes, feeling more and more calm, at which point the neighbors changed the tape and put on something much more jarring. Okay, I thought, I will simply be present with this as well, and gradually got myself into that frame of mind, continuing the meditation. Immediately, they changed the tape again to something so dreadful it must have been invented as a torture device by the CIA (if you do not cooperate, we will put the tape back on; *no, no, I'll tell you everything!*) and quadrupled the volume. That put me over the edge, and I completely lost it, at which point (in what felt like a gesture of the most utterly cynical mockery) they turned the music off.

What would a Master have to say about it? Why do I not have a Master, a Christ? There are graces God can choose to grant or withhold – why are we supposed to believe that the God who forever withholds them is a loving God? *What is going on here?*

I think we should be told.

*   *   *

Yahweh Saboath, the God of Israel, says this to all
the exiles deported from Jerusalem to Babylon:
...Work for the good of the city to which I have exiled
you; pray to Yahweh on its behalf, since on its wel-
fare yours depends.... For Yahweh says this: When
the seventy years granted to Babylon are over, I shall
intervene on your behalf and fulfill my favorable
promise to you by bringing you back to this place.
Yes, I know what plans I have in mind for you,
Yahweh declares, plans for peace, not for disaster,
to give you a future and a hope. When you call to
me and come and pray to me, I shall listen to you.
When you search for me, you will find me; when you
search wholeheartedly for me, I shall let you find me.
(Jeremiah 29:4,7,10-14)

*   *   *

There was a future and a hope after all (God is great). I found a
place to move to, essentially a tiny, one-room box on the flat roof of the
WFP warehouse. There was an even smaller box across the roof with
toilet and shower inside. Down a flight of metal stairs was the door
to the street; the next door, fifty yards away, was the one to my office.

As the packers were doing their work removing me from the apartment from hell, the people upstairs had their hi-fi on at concert-hall
volume, the renovators had a band saw going in the Congolese apartment next door and were pounding on my wall with sledgehammers,
the parrot posted by the neighbors just outside my bedroom window
was EEEEEEKing, cars were lined up outside honking their horns for
someone to lean out their balconies and shout down to them, it was
absolute bedlam. I was so content to be going.

I think the new place is going to be okay, though I could have slept
in North Station without trouble last night, I was so wiped out. Still,

I consider it a good sign that I was able to sleep without earplugs for the first time in a year. There is a parrot in some garret within earshot, but it makes chortling, experimental parrot sounds (let's see what happens if I try *this* – gurgle, trill, tweet!), and doesn't just EEEEEK at me from inside my head. Otherwise, there are mostly the night sounds of generators across the way, nothing special, lots of sky and clouds to watch from my enormous terrace, the backs of two blocks of apartment buildings to check out once I unpack my binoculars. Lots of reorganizing to do, but the basics are out of boxes and within reach; and Bete, the woman who keeps my premises organized, is resourceful when it comes to making do. Part of me proceeds gingerly, not quite able to believe it is going to work, too gun-shy from this last year. Watch this space.

*   *   *

I was sitting in my office half an hour ago when I began to be aware of raised voices outside my door, then a gunshot, then more raised voices, then another gunshot. By this time I had gotten the door locked and retreated behind the filing cabinet. After quite a lot of further commotion, things got back to what we laughingly describe as *normal* around here. Apparently, a couple of the security guards had been drinking, got into an argument, and decided to fire off some shots for the sake of emphasis. For no particularly good reason, nobody got killed. The worst offender got hauled off somewhere – will he be back tomorrow to settle scores?

As I think I have said before, Luanda is a hard place to relax.

*   *   *

"Bandits" outside Chongoroi killed two people from the Santa Barbara Foundation – a young German doctor and a Zimbabwean deminer – plus two police and a local official. In trying to get the dead German doctor home, they found he was too tall for the casket that had been waiting outside my office door, so there was some thought of cutting off the lower part of his legs and chucking them in after the rest of him. There was a fire at the clinic where the body has been staying, though, so the power and refrigeration went off and whatever happened over the next day or so led them to wonder if they could get the corpse into the coffin even without legs. The parents, monitoring all this via unreliable phone lines from Hamburg, have proposed cremation; but there are no facilities for this except for the ELF incinerator, which you can use only if you get all kinds of special permission and they clean out whatever an oil company normally incinerates. Everyone hopes that when the coffin finally arrives in Germany on Tuesday the parents aren't tempted to have a last look at their boy. Wherever the boy himself is, you hope they have a loving sense of humor there.

*   *   *

Sometimes things get in a bumpy groove. I went to the clinic on schedule for my glycemia test,[9] and when the technician finally showed up 40 minutes later, was told they didn't have the reagent. Then I went to Air France, who just laughed at the thought they might have seats out of Luanda anytime near the end of the month. No traffic was moving on the Marginal, so we sat there steaming, the air conditioning broken on the car. Then there was a shot, and a policeman with a gun chasing a kid along the other curb. When he and several security guards caught the kid, they kicked him in the balls, knocked him down, and began beating him. The traffic started moving and we went on to Sabena, which has canceled all flights in and out of Luanda, including the one I was leaving on, and doesn't know what happens next.

I guess I had a better morning than the kid, anyway.

---

[9] By the end of my posting in Angola, the stress of being there had pushed my blood sugar levels into the diabetic range, and the doctors were keeping track of developments. Once I was out of the country, things got back to normal (not *normal*) again.

*   *   *

There was an eleven-year-old girl who lived behind a container at Luanda airport. She survived by begging from people walking to their planes. Yesterday, she saw a little, twin-engine WFP plane sitting in its parking area full of likely almsgivers. She walked toward the plane, arms outstretched in a begging gesture, hoping someone would reach out the door with money. The pilot tried to wave her away, but she kept walking, gesturing. Then the propeller cut both her arms off, and she bled to death.

All over Luanda, we could hear the pilot, badly shaken, calling on the radio: "Sierra Gulf, we have a major incident here at the airport; one person dead." Then the WFP disaster machinery kicked in, and the logisticians took over. We are getting uncomfortably good at this kind of thing.

Chapter 12
TAJIKISTAN
JUNE 1998

In 1998, I made it out of Angola through a transfer to Islamabad, Pakistan, where the World Food Program had a regional office. I was there for two years. Early on, I visited Tajikistan with my boss, Bronek Syznalski, in order to review the WFP program there.

We got lucky going to Dushanbe, Tajikistan's capital. The U.N. has a formidable logistics operation underway in response to May's awful earthquake in Afghanistan, so planes and helicopters are criss-crossing the region with relief workers and supplies. You turn up at an airport and get on whatever is flying.

This meant we could take a little U.N. Beechcraft direct from Islamabad to Dushanbe and return by Tajik Air cargo helicopter from Dushanbe to Faizabad – the airstrip in Afghanistan at the heart of the disaster zone – and then another Beechcraft through Peshawar to Islamabad. If this sounds complicated, consider the "normal" alternative: Pakistan Airways from Islamabad to Lahore, a long wait for a change of planes to Tashkent, then an Uzbek Air flight the next day to Termez, in southern Uzbekistan, and a three-hour trip by road from there to Dushanbe. You reverse this coming home.

The improvisations may not have been wholly sensible, especially the trip back. U.N. personnel are prohibited from flying scheduled flights on Tajik Air since their maintenance is so sloppy, but the unscheduled helicopter seemed too good to pass up. (The idea had never occurred to anyone, so it hadn't been prohibited.) We stopped worrying when they pointed us toward a chopper all polished and tidy, saying this one had been used the previous day to take the President somewhere. We started worrying again when they changed their minds and put us on the next chopper down the line, an old Russian clunker with peeling paint and a discouraged air. We made it, though.

The Russian influence is still everywhere in Tajikistan – in aircraft, faces, language. I had never realized how thoroughly colonized the Soviet Socialist Republics had been, but the story I hear at someone's birthday party from a young woman named Olga helps fill in the gaps. Olga's Russian grandparents had thought Siberia was the end of the line when they were sent there in the '30s. Later, though, when Moscow decided to expand cotton production in the Tajik Socialist Republic, the grandparents got packed up again and shipped to a kolkhoz near Kurgan-Tyube to dig irrigation canals.

Then came the war, and slow starvation. One day, Grandma got caught taking a handful of wheat home to feed Olga's mother. They put Grandma away for five years. Grandpa died. Olga's mother was taken in by neighbors. She survived. Later came Olga, who grew up with no prospects in a poor Russian workers' family.

Even so, she was among the lords and masters. In a colonialism similar to that of the Portuguese in Africa, even Russian laborers had precedence over the natives. The colonists didn't bother with Tajik, which fewer than 4% of the Russians here speak; instead, the Tajiks (at least those who wanted jobs or education) learned Russian. Today, seven years after "independence," the signs around town are still in Cyrillic script, and you hear as much Russian as Tajik on the street.

Tajikistan has been conquered before. In *The Lost Heart of Asia*, a wonderful book about the region, Colin Thubron notes, "For two thousand years Central Asia was the womb of terror, where an implacable queue of barbarian races waited to impel one another into history": Scythians, Huns, Avars, Magyars, Pechenegs, the swift-riding Mongols ("Only their stench, it was said, gave warning of their coming"), Tamerlane. The Russians were just the most recent.

Attila, Genghis Khan, Tamerlane. There is so much romance in simply being in such a place. To the north of Dushanbe is Tashkent, to the northwest Samarkand (the very name "a heart-stealing sound" for Thubron). The distance between Islamabad and Dushanbe is only four hundred miles, but the tortuous complexities of the journey are a reminder that along the way you have crossed some great divide into unknown lands. "Central Asia..."

The tradition of violence remains. In 1992-1993, just after independence, civil war left 50,000 people dead and 700,000 displaced, either within Tajikistan or as refugees in neighboring countries. The war has continued at lower levels of intensity since, and there was a brief firefight in the hills above the WFP office the week before we got there.

The U.N. has not been immune. A few months back, a U.N. woman was kidnapped by one of the military factions and then killed when soldiers came to rescue her. We have an 8:00 curfew now, which means I have to leave the birthday party before hearing the end of Olga's story. On the way back to the WFP guest flat, a security officer (described still as "KGB") joins us in the car to see that mafiosi don't get us, or bandits, or factions in search of more U.N. hostages. Under the circumstances, we are glad for the company.

The city is not in good shape. On the drive back, we pass piles of uncollected garbage. Along the roadside, a family is out late selling skirts and slacks – all the clothes they're not wearing – to collect enough money for food. Cows graze in the parks. A woman in one of the flats in our building has sold every piece of furniture except her piano, which she refuses to part with. (She sleeps on the floor but has her music.) An opera singer and an airline pilot work for WFP as food aid monitors, our driver is a former economist with the State Planning Commission, and the deputy WFP director's cook is an M.D. Everyone is struggling.

Well, not everyone. As has happened in Russia, the vacuum caused by the collapse of communism has been filled by mafiosi. The big money is in the aluminum plant and the cotton fields, and the folks who control those sectors are the ones who drive Mercedes, vacation on the Riviera, and fly off to Israel when they need quality medical care. The people who work in the plant and the fields seldom get paid, but they work anyway, out of inertia and fear and lack of alternatives.

It is not a whole lot better when you do get paid. A month's work picking cotton earns you perhaps $3.50, almost enough to buy four pounds of meat. Teachers and bureaucrats get about the same.

In such a place, WFP's role is to try to ease the pain. We currently provide food rations to more than a half-million people. Most of these are retirees, who found with independence that their monthly pensions had effectively disappeared. We have a lot of women and children on our rolls too, husbandless and fatherless in the aftermath of the civil war. What happens to them when we leave?

Somewhere along his journey, not so far from Dushanbe, Colin Thubron asked a young girl what she wanted to do after she finished school. "[She turned and] walked away. 'I'll be a young woman, then a mother, then an old woman....' Her walk slowed to a dark saunter, and she looked back suddenly over her shoulder. '...Then a corpse.'"

It could have been Olga speaking, or most of her Tajik counterparts.

We finished our business and left, catching the chopper and the Beechcraft and making it back to Islamabad. The next day, violent fighting broke out in the suburbs of Dushanbe. The day after that, everyone on board a Tajik presidential helicopter (the one we hadn't taken?) was badly burned when the thing fell out of the sky. In some ways, being here isn't that different from being in Angola.

Chapter 13
PAKISTAN
1998-2000

When I moved to Pakistan, I was joined by Muff (née
Constance – the unfortunate nickname had been be-
stowed in childhood by her brother), a college love I'd
grown close to again after our respective marriages
failed. At the end of our two years in Islamabad, we
left on planes going in different directions and never
saw each other again. Life is not uncomplicated.

Early morning. Rude and raucous noises proceed from the ledge
outside my bathroom window. A cold yellow eye studies me from the
other side of the screen. "You are only a Common Myna," I explain to
the eye, "but you should still be able to speak. Repeat after me: I AM A
STUPID BIRD." AWK, says the myna, and with an outraged fluffing
of feathers loops its way to a branch of a nearby banana tree.

I know this is a Common Myna – and not, say, a Bank Myna, or a
Chestnut-Headed Tit-Babbler – from the pictures in my Collins bird
book. The cover left the printers saying "Birds of India," but between
there and Mr. Books in Islamabad someone pasted a sticker across
"India." The book is now called "Birds of PAKISTAN and Indian Sub-
Continent." (Urdu is sparing in its use of articles.) Is such an impulse
commercial or political?

We are certainly not India-lovers here. A couple of weeks ago,
Pakistan test-fired its new Ghauri missile, a counter to an Indian
missile called the Prithvi. The President announced that this

peace-keeping measure would allow Pakistan to "defend its sacred soil" while keeping a watch on "the enemy's sinister designs." With a fluffing of feathers that would shame my Myna, officials then pointed out that the original Ghauri was a 12th century Muslim emperor who defeated in battle the original Prithvi, the Hindu ruler of Delhi at the time.

Sophisticated technologies of destruction are hardly a monopoly of the military. I was talking with a Pakistani colleague about a national map he had produced for us, the districts color-coded by degree of social development. Many of the worst-off areas are along the Afghan border. "These are real tribal people," observed my colleague, pointing at the map, "the kind who have rocket launchers and shoot at each other."

The arms are a function of twenty years of warfare in Afghanistan. A lot of the stuff was originally supplied by the West so the mujahideen could have at the Russians. Now the leftover weaponry is available to keep the Afghan civil war alive, or for hire to anyone nearby with a grievance. Last month, when ill will spun out of control between Sunnis and Shias in Hangu (a town in remotest North West Frontier Province), accounts were settled with mortars, rocket launchers, and other heavy weapons. Official figures (probably understated) claim that 26 people died and 50 were injured.

Each part of the country seems to have its own form of violence. An average of thirty or forty people die every year in bomb blasts in the Punjab (ninety died in 1996); and in Sindh, especially in Karachi, sectarian shootings are an almost daily event. Such episodes have a long history: Sultan Ghauri was murdered in a vendetta by tribesmen that he thought he had conquered.

Some of the saddest of the violence stories involve lovers who cross communal lines. Riffat, a young Pathan woman from Karachi, eloped earlier this year with Kanwar, a Mohajir. Claiming that Riffat had been kidnapped, Pathans roamed the streets of Karachi in a spasm of violence that left two people dead and at least eight seriously injured. Riffat's family then convened a jirga (a gathering of tribal elders), which sentenced her to death for leaving (whether willingly or not, the disgrace would be the same) with a man not of her kind. Kanwar was taken into "protective custody" that proved not so protective – inside a Karachi courthouse on his way to a hearing last month, he was shot by Riffat's relatives. He survived, partly paralyzed, and the two are somewhere in hiding. Last September, another Pathan-Mohajir union ended with both lovers murdered after a jirga found their relationship to be a capital crime. There is enough of this that a local magazine, *Newsline*, devoted its latest cover to "The Price of Love" in a country where "feudal-tribal traditions, religious mores and vendettas conspire to spill the blood" of the Riffats and the Kanwars.

In such a charged environment, no one is exempt. Iranians have been a target in recent months (too Shi'ite in a Sunni land), and four American oil workers were shot on their way to work in Karachi last year. Recently, the Saudi dissident Osama bin Laden called on his followers to attack Americans wherever they might be found. Since bin Laden is reputedly the man responsible for the bombings that killed 24 U.S. servicemen in Saudi Arabia in 1995-96, and since he currently resides just across the border in Afghanistan, the American community here took him seriously. The U.S. Embassy, already surrounded by walls topped with razor wire, blocked nearby streets with concrete barriers and warned Americans in Pakistan to take all possible precautions (vary your route to work; vary the times you travel). When Clinton finally works out a pretext for bombing Afghanistan, we are going to be in big trouble.

This can all seem faintly ridiculous, since on a daily basis, the Pakistanis with whom we deal (at work or at home) are kind and thoughtful to a fault. There could be few places quite so welcoming. And yet, one does get edgy. I walked the block to the covered market the other day, woke up the barber sleeping in his cubicle along the market's outer walls, and settled in for a much-needed haircut. Then I saw the barber in the mirror, approaching with large grin and straight razor, and for a moment the voice of Osama bin Laden was loud in my ears.

*   *   *

Early morning. There is a TAP TAP TAPing abroad in the land. Reluctantly, I climb out of bed and trace the sound to the bathroom window. While I was in Swat, Gulzar, the woman who takes care of the house, took it upon herself to sweep the mynas' nesting materials off the ledge and then to latch the window. The mynas, unreconciled, want in. I open the window. AWK, say the mynas, and retreat to their banana tree.

Gulzar may not have much sympathy for nesting mynas, but she has a lot for us. When we moved in, she was already living (with undefined duties) in the quarters behind the house. She has stayed on to help with cleaning and ironing but seems to feel it her charge to see we are happy and fed. Most evenings, she arrives with a dish of the food she has prepared for her own dinner, vegetables or dal and nan. Mornings, she appears with a particularly fragrant blossom or a necklace of flowers for Muff. When we are sitting in the sunroom at the front of the house, we often look up to find her peering through the screen door, checking to see we're okay.

There is a kind of sweetness at work here that I also saw throughout the trip to Swat, not just in the ways Pakistanis treat visitors, but also in the ways they can treat each other (not counting some of the things noted earlier and below). Our team was looking at Village Development Committees (VDCs) and at the ways these act to implement WFP's natural resource management projects. We found that while the VDCs do go through the motions of planting our trees, what they really want is to build their communities together.

It took a while to find this out. The kinds of meetings a mission like ours has with VDCs are carefully choreographed. We are met at the edge of the village and taken to a room hung with posters showing VDC membership and activities. Often, there are photos of people and trees in various combinations. (The hand-lettered captions can shed something less than light on what these photos represent: "PEBBLES STIRRING THE STAGNATION"; "FUTURE WORRIED OVER PRESENT.") Someone chants a verse from the Koran, the Secretary of the VDC reads out the posters in Pushtu, there is a translation into

English, we ask a few questions, tea appears (usually with cake, biscuits, chicken or fish, and more), then we go walking up the hill to see the trees. There is not a lot of room for freewheeling chat in a dance this formalized.

Once on the hill, though, people loosen up and start talking about things that matter: the village water supply they want to install or a road that needs repair, maybe a river dike to protect their land, schools and clinics, electricity and phones. Although they would like the project to help them out, they do a surprising amount on their own – everywhere we go, there are roads that communities have turned out to build, water tanks they have repaired together, mosques kept rainproof and tidy, all with no need for the WFPs of the world to provide "incentives" in the form of food rations or cash. After decades in and out of African countries where people have come to expect payment for doing such things, I am taken by surprise.

There is a tradition of "ashar" (mutual help) on private holdings as well. In Kohay, we are told how people assemble to harvest wheat or weed tomatoes on each other's land, or pitch in when someone needs a roof repaired. It reminds me of the day all of Wolcott, Vermont, showed up to get the foundation laid for a friend's new house, the rural New England version of "ashar." (Does ashar still exist in Vermont?) There is a lovely alertness here to the needs of one's fellows, and a feeling that some things are just more fun done together.

I wouldn't want to give the impression that the folks in Swat are softies. Swat is one of the tougher areas of North West Frontier Province, whose capital is Peshawar. (The provincial daily paper is *The Frontier Post*, a wonderful name.) When we checked into the Pearl Continental for an overnight in Peshawar on the way to Swat, we were greeted by a large sign: "Weapons cannot be brought inside the hotel premises. Personal Guards or Gunmen are required to deposit their weapons with the Hotel Security. We seek your cooperation." Would you want to be the one to enforce an edict like that?

There can be a certain toughness in the way the project works, too. Activities may have very different effects on different kinds of people. When we close a hillside to grazing in order to plant trees, some people find it easier than others to keep their animals home and buy grass to stall-feed them. In Alamganj, we were told that if the poor had to sell their animals for lack of grazing, they could always go collect pine needles instead. (The needles are sold as packing material for transporting fruit to market, but this seems a poor substitute for the herd of buffalo you once had.)

The people who gain are likely to be the more powerful, who control the land on which the trees are planted. Asked if he would be willing to share his proceeds from the project with the landless, the Chairman of the VDC in Alamganj replied that if Allah had not given land to the poor, what concern was it of his? Not everyone here is equally alert to the needs of his fellows.

Especially if his fellows are women. We noted right away that when the VDC briefings got around to schools, there would be mention of a couple of primary schools for boys and a secondary school for boys, plus a lone primary school for girls. It took us longer to realize that most of the girls' schools were expressions of intent that existed only on paper. Girls play outside until they are seven or eight and then disappear, never to be seen in public again. There are no women on VDCs – in some villages, they can join a project-initiated women's group, to which nobody pays much serious attention.

The project is trying to loosen things up by employing female "community mobilizers" and taking women on excursions to neighboring villages. It isn't easy, though. Toheed Gul, the woman from the project who accompanied us on our rounds, does her work in spite of:

– the resistance of her parents, who initially told her that no girl in their family would ever work outside the home;

– the reluctance of her colleagues to accept her as an equal (or even as a real person);

– the lack of any VDC interest in the women's groups she is trying to establish;

– difficulty in getting her bosses to support those few things the groups can do, such as creating seedling nurseries (which can survive only if the project agrees to buy the seedlings);

– resistance on the part of the community to the idea that women should do such things;

– public denunciation at the mosque during Friday prayers (this has happened) when things get pushed too fast.

Toheed's friends say she looks unhealthy these days and should think of quitting; but when she reports this, there is a look in her eye that says not to hold your breath waiting.

One could begin to disbelieve in Pakistani sweetness; and yet... My last day in Swat, I bag the formal schedule, commandeer an interpreter and driver, and travel unannounced to Kokarai, a project village we haven't seen yet. The VDC doesn't know I'm coming, so I wander the streets talking informally with an ever-growing mob of people. We eventually end up in the community courtyard where men gather for talk and tea. The VDC Chairman has found us by now and sits beside me, but the tone is relaxed, with no need to dwell on the project and its trees.

I ask about a sign on the wall, mysterious writings in Pushtu followed by "A"s and "B+"s. This turns out to be a list of 26 villagers and their blood types, everybody ready to donate blood if needed. Most of what the VDC has done, or has in mind, is a response to local need. They laid claim to the skins of animals slaughtered at Eid, sold them, and paid to send sick villagers to Islamabad and Peshawar for treatment. When a house collapsed in a storm, killing one of the occupants, the VDC made a contribution to the family. Money has been distributed to poor families, and a collection is underway to buy books and shoes for students who couldn't otherwise afford them. Where does the impulse come from for a community to do such things?

There is another poster on the wall, sayings of prominent Islamic teachers. With great seriousness, the Chairman reads me some of these: "Believe in Allah, the Prophet, and in life after death"; "Always control three things: your anger, your tongue, and your heart"; "Don't talk against people in their absence"; "To the extent you can, provide and help."

Provide and help. The penny drops: the source of much of what we have seen on this trip (both the noble and the twisted) is Islam. If a dubious reading of the Koran can keep women shrouded or at home, a deeper reading can move people to extraordinary expressions of caring and generosity. (People can even be led to natural resource management, guided by a quote we saw at one VDC from the works of Masnad Ahmad Bin Humble: "Even on the day of judgment, if you have a branch in your hand plant it at once.") It is no mere formality to start every meeting with the Koran, or to pray five times a day – these things have consequences, and the Kokarai VDC is one. I leave town a little tearful, though I would never admit to such a thing. I guess I have to learn more about Islam.

Back in Islamabad, we enjoy the last days of spring. Walking around our neighborhood, we pass down lanes of jacaranda in full blossom, the trees mirrored in the amethyst sea of petals they have dropped to the ground. Flocks of green parrots roost in the loquat trees. Crested hoopoes hop across emerald lawns in search of grubs. In every open space, marijuana grows wild. I'm not looking forward much to summer here (when temperatures rise into the humid high 110s), but I wouldn't for anything have missed what we've had so far.

*   *   *

I have to learn more about Islam? Maybe the Muslims need to learn more about Islam. According to Karen Armstrong's "History of God," the Koran "stressed the unity of the religious experience of mankind" and taught that "God had sent messengers to every people on the face of the earth," not just the Arabs of 7th century Mecca, requiring Muslims to "recognize the religious aspirations of others." Tell that to any Christian in Pakistan today.

Ten days ago, Bishop John Joseph walked into the courthouse in Sahiwal where Ayub Massih had been condemned to death not long before. Massih was alleged to have spoken favorably of Salman Rushdie, thus blaspheming Islam. Or so said Massih's accuser, a man whose full beard caused the judge to call him a good Muslim and therefore an honest man. Father Joseph had a different slant on things, noting that local Christians had been engaged in a dispute with Muslim landowners and that the action against Massih forced them to abandon the disputed land and flee their village. In a public letter, Joseph wrote that "we must act strongly... without worrying about the sacrifices we shall have to offer. Dedicated persons do not count the cost." He then traveled to Sahiwal to lead a prayer meeting, went from there to the courthouse, and shot himself.

You might think that would have set people to finding ways to heal. You would be wrong. At a memorial service two days later, clashes between police and mourners left three people with bullet wounds, including a young girl. Two days after that, what the Associated Press described as "a mob of Muslim extremists" burned shops and homes in a Christian neighborhood of Faisalabad while Father Joseph was being buried nearby. Christians then attacked the police, who responded with tear gas and beatings. Yesterday, during a series of protests by Christians across the country, there were violent clashes in Rawalpindi and Lahore. Scores of people were injured, more than 100 shops looted, and dozens of vehicles torched.

The strong feelings are not going to go away. During the mob action in Faisalabad, Muslims set Bibles on fire and destroyed pictures of Jesus. According to the law under which Massih was condemned, however, there was nothing blasphemous in so doing. The Penal Code's Section 295-C defines blasphemy this way: "Whoever by words, either spoken or written, or by visible representation, or by any imputation, innuendo, or insinuation, directly or indirectly, defiles the sacred name of the Holy Prophet Muhammad (peace be upon him) shall by punished with death." There are other sections of the law to cover insults to "the religion of any class of persons," presumably even Christians, but the penalties are minimal and no such cases come to mind.

With laws like this, and in an atmosphere like this, any Christian who breathed a defiling word about the Holy Prophet would have to be mad as a hatter, hardly responsible enough for his actions to be sentenced to death. But few think the real issue is blasphemy in any case. Writing in today's *News*, Anees Jillani says, "The laws have become a tool in the hands of a section of the population to crush the religious minorities; if the latter get into any kind of dispute whatsoever with a Muslim, the easiest way to punish the adversary is by accusing him or her of blasphemy. The state machinery takes care of the rest."

According to some reports, more than 200 Christians are now under sentence of death throughout the country for "blasphemy."

A Pakistani Christian of my acquaintance (working class, as are most Christians here) talks of incidents with Muslims: "They say many bad things about Jesus, and I am very angry, but I cannot say anything. If I do, they will tell the police I said bad things about Muhammad, and I will be taken to jail." He hopes for a better life for his children, but assumes that would have to be in some other country. "For a Christian, you can only get good education here if you have much money." There are no more than a couple of million Christians in this country of 140 million, and they are pretty much stuck in a fearful place.

Even Muslims who bear no responsibility for the situation seem not to appreciate its gravity. A Pakistani Muslim (also working class) tells me that he and Christians normally live as brothers. "We drink tea together, and if you come you cannot tell who is Muslim and who is Christian." Only when "outsiders" stir up trouble, he says, do things get nasty.

I doubt that many of his Christian brothers would hold to that view. As things now stand, the accusation by anyone with a long enough beard that you have indirectly insinuated a defilement of the sacred name can land you in a death cell; and "a section of the population" seems unreluctant to take advantage of the fact. Pakistan is hardly the first country to mistreat its minorities, but the situation here is no prettier for that. After a lifetime of struggle, Bishop Joseph apparently decided that the only way to call attention to this was to shoot himself.

Unfortunately, his timing was awful. India conducted five nuclear weapons tests this week, and Pakistan is probably hours away from an equivalent, "appropriate response." People have other things on their minds than religious tolerance. Yesterday, my Christian acquaintance talked from deep within himself as he described the fasting and mourning and protests planned in Father Joseph's honor, an almost unique opportunity for Pakistan's Christians to carry their case to the world. Both he and I knew, though, that nobody was going to pay much attention; and the look in his eye as we talked was terrible to see.

PAKISTAN

*   *   *

Islamabad Week (August 1998)

Friday 14th. Take Muff to airport. Spend day trying to imagine how I will keep from perishing of boredom in her absence. Perhaps duties will emerge in connection with the fact that Bronek is on leave, and I'm acting in his place as head of the regional office.

Saturday 15th. Pakistan government secretly puts Mohammad Saddiq Odeh (seized at Karachi airport earlier in week) on plane back to Nairobi. Turns out later that Odeh had admitted under "intensive questioning" (what David Foster Wallace called "technical interviews"?) that he was involved in the bombing of the U.S. embassy in Nairobi on the 7th[10] and that the whole episode was sponsored by Osama bin Laden, our neighbor across the border in Afghanistan.

Sunday 16th. In worldwide exclusive, the Islamabad-based *News* breaks the story on page 1.

Monday 17th. U.S. Embassy/Islamabad announces that all official American families and all but "essential" staff will leave Pakistan. At afternoon meeting with unofficial Americans, U.S. ambassador distributes statement urging the rest of us to "consider seriously departing Pakistan" but won't say why.

Tuesday 18th. 200 U.S. Embassy staff and dependents leave on chartered plane from heavily guarded military airport outside Islamabad. U.N. in turmoil – what do they know that we don't know?

Wednesday 19th. Nonstop high-level U.N. security meetings; urgent messages between Islamabad, Rome, New York. People beginning to behave in strange ways: my colleague J especially at dangerous stress point.

Thursday 20th. U.S. and British intelligence deliver urgent warnings that all foreigners in Afghanistan, especially Americans and people working for non-Muslim NGOs, are under serious threat. U.N. orders staff in Afghanistan to gather at guesthouses in four main cities, tries to think what to do next. No sign of J, who has decided

---

[10] An explosives-laden truck was detonated outside the embassy, damaging it, collapsing a nearby building, and incinerating a commuter bus. 213 people were killed and 4,000 injured. 11 were killed in a simultaneous bombing at the U.S. embassy in Dar-es-Salaam.

that the Saudi Pak Tower, where we have our offices, is the next main target for international terrorism and refuses to come to work. In late evening, President Clinton launches Cruise missile attacks against al-Qaeda bases in Afghanistan.

<u>Friday 21st</u>. Three-hour meeting of Combined U.N. Security Management Team, attended by heads of all U.N. agencies here (including me as Acting Regional Manager for WFP). Priority is to get people out of Afghanistan. Two U.N. staff shot in Kabul last night; both stable. Taliban cooperating with evacuation airlift. All international staff in Pakistan being moved by air or armed convoy to Islamabad. U.N. offices closed until further notice, along with International School and U.N. Club. J and family book flight to Bangkok on Sunday.

<u>Saturday 22nd</u>. Convoy arrived with U.N. staff from Peshawar at 3:30 this morning; first planes in from Afghanistan last night. The Italian U.N. staffer shot yesterday in Kabul died this morning. There are reports of demonstrators headed toward the U.S. Embassy and Saudi Pak Tower in Islamabad, but nothing happens. In the absence of real action, the BBC runs the same film over and over of someone burning an American flag somewhere. U.N. staff under 8 p.m.-5 a.m. curfew, "restricted movement" for rest of day. I'm out in the office car taking supplies to staff in their homes and trying to raise morale. Long security meeting in afternoon. J and family now joined in plans for Bangkok flight by K and A.

<u>Sunday 23rd</u>. My dining room has become the WFP Command Center: mobile phone for incoming calls, mobile phone for outgoing calls, two-way radio for when the mobiles fail (the government shuts the system down as soon as real trouble starts, so organizers can't use it for communications). Nonstop calls to Rome, Nairobi, Dushanbe, Paris, Vermont and WFP staff all over Islamabad, though everything remains peaceful and people are mostly doing their spring cleaning and visiting neighbors. Js, K, A, and their three dogs, cat, and parrot leave for airport in three-vehicle convoy, all movements closely coordinated with U.N. security officer.

Are we bored yet?[11]

---

[11] Gradually, things calmed down and we returned to what passed for normalcy in Pakistan in those days.

PAKISTAN

*   *   *

The UN has decided that its various agencies should cooperate with each other (one of those headquarters-generated ideas that sound lovely at headquarters but make little or no sense in the real world), and the FAO representative here is trying to promote forms of cooperation. I went to his office earlier in the week to discuss their request that WFP convene a meeting to present a Working Paper to the Pakistan U.N. Agencies' Development Group's ACC-inspired Thematic Group on Food Security's Task Force on Emergency Preparedness, Early Warning and Response. (I did not make that up.) This is something that my boss Bronek got us into way last year ("Oh, yes, emergency preparedness sounds nice, we believe in that") without quite realizing what the implications would be. Our meeting was to puzzle out the implications.

The conversation rapidly confirmed my assumption that this was all vaporous U.N. language, that none of it made any sense, and that the more we tried to pretend to take it seriously, the more time we would spend in meetings accomplishing nothing. Needless to say, the FAO Representative saw things otherwise, wanting quickly to take the next step into discussion of coordinated U.N. mechanisms and modalities for appropriate response to hypothetical scenarios of emergencies such as earthquakes, floods, and droughts.

Look, I said, there is a prolonged, serious drought *now* underway in the country, probably a consequence of La Niña. The newspapers are writing about the potential loss of a million tons of grain in this year's crop. Rather than talking in the abstract about mechanisms and modalities, why don't we devote our meeting to discussing the drought: what do we know about it? what might we think of doing in response? what else do we need to know to make informed choices? beyond what our agencies would do anyway on their own, is there anything useful we could do through cooperating with each other? We might end up with U.N. system mechanisms and modalities, or we might not. At least we would have come to an approach on the basis of looking at a real situation.

Shock on the FAO side of the table, dropping of jaws, eyes widening. Oh no, no, we couldn't do that, no. That would be premature until we have identified mechanisms and modalities.

Well, gee, I don't know, say I, it may depend in part on how grave we expect the consequences of the drought to be for agriculture in Pakistan, and how long we can wait before addressing the problem. What is FAO's analysis of the situation?

Um, well, um, uh, well (says the FAO Representative), I think we have a La Niña Working Group in Rome or Delhi or somewhere, and they may be putting maps together for the subcontinent, but I don't think they have a map yet for Pakistan, we can try to find out.

Let me get this straight, I think: is it really that the Pakistan office of the U.N. Food and Agriculture Organization has given no thought to the implications for Pakistan's food and agriculture of a severe, current drought, and rather than being willing to discuss this is hassling WFP to produce a Working Paper for the local U.N. Agencies' Development Group's ACC-inspired Thematic Group on Food Security's Task Force on Emergency Preparedness, Early Warning and Response, in order (following agreement on a Proposal for necessary studies, their funding to be arranged in ways yet to be determined and their implementation to then be turned over to a team of consultants yet to be identified and hired, who would take an unknown amount of time to produce a report for endorsement by the Task Force for consideration by the Thematic Group for submission to the Development Group for appropriate action, probably consisting of the convening of further meetings) to move toward mechanisms and modalities for a coordinated response to hypothetical emergency scenarios?

Yes, I realize, it really is this way. What would be the Buddhist response to such an understanding?

*　　　　*　　　　*

According to an editorial in the current *Newsline*, "1998 will go down in Pakistan's history as the year when the candle of hope flickered in the stormy winds. Never, in its fifty years, have the people been so overcome with despair... Never before have so many lost faith in the future of this country – and its leaders." *The Friday Times* suggests that Pakistanis are increasingly asking "the following anguished questions: what the hell is going on, where the hell are we going and how the hell do we get out of this bloody mess?" And yesterday's *News* reports that a poll by Gallup International finds Pakistanis to be sharply less hopeful about the future than they were a year ago.

(Even so, everything is relative: Pakistan still ranks as "the ninth most hopeful country in the world," or at least ninth among the countries surveyed by Gallup. Either *Newsline* and the *FT* are overstating the case or it is a gloomy world.)

Whatever the exact calculus of hope and despair, 1998 brought Pakistan some memorable moments. Towering over all else was Pakistan's detonation of nuclear weapons on May 28 and 30, which followed the Indian tests of May 11 and 13. The West's military think tanks put their war gamers to work modeling the possible events that could follow from any serious confrontation between India and Pakistan once the "devices" are turned into usable bombs; the outcome, every time, was nuclear war. (What are the odds this will happen in the year, four months, and twenty-nine days before I leave?)

The immediate result was declaration of a national state of emergency, suspension of fundamental civil rights, imposition of sanctions by the United States, the freezing of foreign currency accounts, effective devaluation of the rupee, and the fall of stock values to record lows on the Karachi exchange.

Much of the remainder of the year was spent with the country on (or quietly over) the brink of default on foreign loans. The IMF and the World Bank talked bailout, but on the usual conditions: increased taxes and utility bills for the poor coupled with cutbacks in government spending (except for the counterpart funds needed to keep World Bank projects going).

On the political front, Prime Minister Nawaz Sharif ousted the Chief Justice of the Supreme Court, the President, and the Chief of Army Staff, replacing them with his own men. He then set to work introducing shariah law and undercutting the vestigial powers of his puppet president. Yesterday's review of 1998 in the *News* refers to him as "the democratically-elected-PM-turned-civilian-dictator."

Corruption reached new heights, with the Prime Minister leading the way. Details could not always be confirmed, but it was generally believed that Nawaz defaulted on huge loans, moved his dollars out of the country the night before foreign exchange holdings were frozen, bought up valuable properties in London, and used government funds to improve his residence near Lahore (including an "office" with three kitchens, three drawing rooms, a swimming pool, a zoo, and a surrounding lake). For her part, Benazir Bhutto, the leader of the opposition, spent the year fighting charges of corruption and money laundering in Swiss and Pakistani courts.

The crisis in "civil society" intensified in many ways, according to *The Friday Times*: "In continuing deterioration of law and order. In rising sectarianism, ethnicity and regionalism. In the breakdown of civil utilities and amenities. In the erosion of the administrative system. In violence and armed conflict. In mass criminalization and alienation of the masses. In a rising graph of mental disorders, drug abuse, rape, kidnapping and outright terrorism. [In] the rise of criminal and religious mafias..."

Meanwhile, from next door in Afghanistan, the Taliban kept sending ripples across the border. Villagers in Pakistan's Northwest Frontier Province began to administer Taliban-style justice without recourse to the niceties of the law, and an ever-wider area along the border became an unfriendly zone for foreigners. As one of only three countries in the world to recognize the Taliban government, Pakistan got on ever-edgier terms with the countries in the region (Iran, Tajikistan) that are trying to bring the Taliban down. And when the Taliban's most controversial guest, Osama bin Laden, came under fire from U.S. Cruise missiles on August 20, the Pakistan government was hard-pressed to explain away its apparent advance knowledge of the bombings, as well as the several missiles that missed their targets and came down in Pakistani territory.

Most ominously, the carnage continued in Kashmir: "India Reports 34 Killed by Rebels Over Kashmir"; "52 Killed in Exchanges of Fire Along Kashmir Frontier"; "Eight Die in Indian Kashmir Attack";

"33 More Martyred in Indian Firing on Free Kashmir Villages"; "India, Pakistan Exchange Fire for Third Day"; "Border Clashes Intensify in Kashmir." This is the context into which nuclear capabilities have now been introduced. According to the director of the Carnegie Endowment's Nonproliferation Project, "If both India and Pakistan deployed nuclear weapons, I think it would almost certainly lead to a nuclear exchange in combat." This is likely to take some time to materialize, but people here may soon begin to absorb the enormity of what is coming.

Have a nice '99...

*   *   *

This is a scary country just now. Tired of relentless exposure of corruption and dirty deeds in high places, the Government is trying to put the independent press out of business. The paper we read – *The News* – is down to a handful of pages (fortunately, the sports page survives so far) since the government has cut off their supplies of newsprint. An Urdu-language paper published by the same group is under similar pressure. The government has insisted that 16 of the group's staff be fired, including the editor of *The News*, who has herself received death threats. *The News* says it may only be able to hold out for a day or two more, and will then have to suspend publication.

You have to worry about the editor, since you don't lightly piss this government off. Three men accused of involvement in an alleged attempt to assassinate the Prime Minister were killed in police custody yesterday. According to the authorities, they were being transported from Lahore to Multan under heavy police guard when armed men tried to free them. In what should have been one of the shootouts of the decade, the three accused were killed "in the crossfire." Remarkably, none of the attackers and no policemen suffered any injuries, and the attackers quickly disappeared. Unfortunately, there is a lot of this going around; it even has a name: "custodial murder."

The Government is looking for other ways as well to achieve efficient justice. President Tarar yesterday invoked an article of the constitution allowing military courts throughout the country to try "hardened criminals" involved in various offences (including pissing off the government?), and to award "exemplary punishments." This is an extension of a system recently introduced in Sindh Province that has been roundly denounced as a crude violation of civil rights. The Supreme Court has questioned the validity of these courts, which tend to interpret "exemplary punishments" as meaning swift hanging, but that is not slowing the process down. To remind the military whose side they are on as they assume their judicial functions, the Prime Minister on Friday raised all their salaries.

In case the military should miss any transgressions, the Taliban are being unleashed. The government of NWFP Province recently endorsed the application of shariah law in two districts, to be overseen largely by Taliban fundamentalists. This has already led to summary executions of people found guilty of crimes by Taliban "courts." In Hangu District, people have been warned that Taliban enforcers will today conduct house-to-house searches, with the intent of seizing and burning "evil gadgets" such as television sets and dish antennas. Women found without veils and anyone making music will be severely dealt with. If the government eventually succeeds in passing the proposed Fifteenth Amendment, which would extend shariah law to the entire country, Islamabad may be next.

To give a human face to the prevailing nastiness, there is the story of Hamaira and Mehmood Butt, who made the mistake of marrying without the approval of Hamaira's father. Dad, a member of the Punjab parliament and one of the country's largest landowners, is another of those people you don't want to cross. Mehmood was taken to a police station and beaten for two days. Prudently, he left for the U.S., where his father had a business. To keep Humaira at home and out of trouble, she was put in a full-body plaster cast for three months. She also had her thumbprint forcibly placed on a marriage certificate, backdated to a month before her wedding to Mehmood.

The couple recently got back together, but only briefly. Humaira's family brought various criminal charges against them and had Humaira restricted to a locked city shelter in Karachi. The Sindh High Court ruled that she should be allowed her freedom, and she and Mehmood booked a flight to the States. When they went to the airport on Thursday, they were jumped by a group of men who turned out to be police. They haven't been seen since. Today's *News* editorializes that the police "have engaged in an act of crime which at the least amounts to kidnapping and could, in the worst case scenario, end in murder." You can understand why *The News* is in trouble, and Mehmood and Humaira, and Pakistan.

The other major news this morning is that the "Paris Club" of major donors is rescheduling $3.3 billion in outstanding external debt as "a positive contribution to Pakistan's adjustment and reform efforts." This supplements several hundred million dollars in recent loans from the World Bank and IMF. Naturally, it is of paramount importance to ensure that Western banking and commercial interests in Pakistan are protected, and that the World Bank and IMF are free to go about their business. Do you suppose, though, that any of these guys have considered where more adjustment and reform efforts along current lines are likely to lead?

It is, of course, a rhetorical question...

*   *   *

I watched a butterfly die this morning. Early on, thinking of the reasons why Muff chose not to interfere in the death of her dog – not to have her put down – I decided it wasn't my role to save the butterfly from suffering. I just watched, and breathed.

The whole process took a long hundred minutes. For the first half of this, the butterfly lay or flopped around on the step outside the sunroom door. It was old enough or sick enough not to make a serious attempt to fly off anywhere. It seemed to want to perch someplace, but didn't have the energy to hold on to anything. The milky green tint of its wings had turned dusty.

Finally, the butterfly slipped off the step into a patch of grass and weeds and dead leaves. It didn't want to be there but couldn't climb out again, and flying was quite hopeless by now. It mostly lay still, only moving (and then just a feeble flapping of wings) when an ant would pass by and poke at it to see what manner of thing this might be.

Abruptly, for no reason I could discern, the ants decided this was no longer a butterfly, but food. From all around, they swarmed to it, dozens of them. The butterfly began to flutter seriously now and cast its legs about, but its body had become too heavy for it to move. I couldn't see well what was happening beneath the wings, but the ants must have been tearing pieces from the butterfly because it began to convulse, curling desperately in on itself again and again, convulsion all that remained in its power through the agony. This went on for perhaps twenty minutes.

That is when I did my breathing. I breathed in the convulsions, and breathed out the light and space the butterfly was headed for, and felt helpless and ignorant. What forms would a butterfly see at the end of its tunnel? What could anyone outside do to ease its passage? Breathe in; breathe out.

I don't know exactly when the butterfly died, since the agitation of the ants gave the wings an occasional flutter even when there could have been no life left in it. The dismembering of the butterfly had started even while it was alive, and the process was complete within a half hour of its death. Wing sections disappeared into the bushes, and pieces of body, and eventually there was nothing left at all.

*   *   *

A couple of weeks ago, a man in Lahore named Shahbaz found that a financial deal he had with a local drummer seemed to be falling through. Shahbaz decided that the problem lay in a friendship between the drummer and a local young woman, a prominent classical dancer. Shahbaz went to her home and shot her to death. Her father – one of Pakistan's leading painters – intervened, and Shahbaz killed him too.

After Shahbaz was apprehended, someone asked him why he hadn't finished things off by shooting himself as well. He replied that as a Muslim he couldn't have done that, since "Islam prohibits suicide."

*   *   *

I have a few free minutes, the first in what seems like weeks. I don't know where these grotesquely dense periods appear from, but they descend like the third painting in Thomas Cole's sequence on the stages of life, the one where you are in a boat plummeting through the rapids with no higher ambition than to stay afloat.

As daily context, all around is total breakdown in the way traffic works, leading to debris and wrecks scattered along the streets of Islamabad where people have barreled into each other running lights and passing in hopeless ways. Ever since I first went to Ethiopia in 1961, I have realized that traffic patterns are a rich metaphor for how a society is working. The dramatic deterioration of driving here over the past year mirrors the deterioration of Pakistan, 10-12 cars running (at great speed) each red light, people shooting it out over minor indignities, the government becoming more fascistic with each passing day.

Not to mention Bill Clinton and Osama bin Laden taking potshots at each other just over our heads (so far).

*   *   *

Last week, a woman named Samia Imran fled from Peshawar to Lahore to escape a brutal husband. When her parents came after her to order her home, she retreated to a refuge run by Asma Jehangir, a noted civil rights activist. If this sounds like just another sad domestic story, hardly of mortal import, remember Riffat and Kanwar and Hamaira and Mehmood. After all, this *is* Pakistan.

Samia agreed to see her mother at the refuge; but when the mother came, she brought with her a man who shot Samia dead. The man in turn was shot by a security guard, but Mom and Dad melted into the shadows of Lahore and haven't been seen since. As in the Hamaira case, Dad is a man of substance, not easily rendered invisible. (Among other rather public things, he is President of the Sarhad Chamber of Commerce and Industry.) And Mom is reported to be a prominent physician. Darn, though, the police just can't lay their hands on them for now.

In Sarhad Chamber of Commerce circles, such acts may be taken for granted. In Islamabad, however, the backlash was immediate. Shafqat Mahmood, one of several outraged columnists in yesterday's *News*, wrote: "I am numb when I read that a mother watches, without emotion, without any obvious distress, her daughter being killed.... After the deed is done, she does not stop or break down on seeing her daughter collapse in a pool of blood. She, as the papers like to put it, makes good her escape." And the idea that the murder might somehow have been an act of Islamic obligation was rejected out of hand – seeking divorce is a basic right of Muslim women, not a capital crime.

Back in Peshawar, though, Mom and Dad's buddies demanded that Asma (Asma!) be summarily hanged. In street demonstrations, they accused Asma of crimes such as promoting Western values, putting women on the path of immorality, ridiculing the institution of marriage, and challenging Islam. Samia's complicity in this was assumed to be persuasive reason for her parents to have her killed.

According to today's paper, a lawyer for Samia's parents is now seeking to bring formal charges of murder against Asma and her colleague Hina Jillani. The lawyer quotes Mom (perhaps the puzzled police should ask the lawyer where Mom is...) as saying that, well, yes, her driver took a shot at Samia and was then killed running from the scene. Still, this was all due to a "conspiracy" hatched by Asma and Hina; and the killing of the driver by the security guard proves they wanted to eliminate an important witness. Honest, that's the way the parents' story goes. Perhaps the most startling aspect of the whole episode is that they should expect anyone to take them seriously.

One greatly fears the next chapter.

Appropriately, I spent the last two days at a workshop sponsored by the Center for Peace and Pluralism, an embryonic institution run by our friend Kamran. This particular meeting gathered a dozen people, mostly academics (and all, except for me, Pakistani), to give shape to a book on ways to support pluralism in Pakistan. The hope is that by nurturing pluralistic ways of viewing the world, the Center can help temper the violent, intolerant forces, the malign kinds of "single vision," that led to Hamia's death (and that threaten to tear Pakistan apart along various brittle fault lines).

Kamran and his colleagues believe that pluralism is a subcontinental legacy – or was, at least during parts of the Moghul era and after. In those lost times, Hindus and Muslims (and whoever else was around) could live together, share heroes (and sometimes gods), in a rich and creative interpenetration of "multiple truth claims."

That wasn't working well by the time of Independence, when Muslims felt they needed a state of their own. Still, in the 1950s and 1960s, Pakistani textbooks could refer to Gandhi as a "man of peace" (he is now viewed as an anti-Islamic sectarian) and find historical greatness in people other than Muslims. In schools, students were offered "comparative religion" rather than "Koranic studies." At least within limits, there was a certain fluidity in the way the world was viewed.

This didn't last. Hostilities with India became more entrenched with the Indo-Pakistani Wars of 1965 and 1971 (during the second of which East Pakistan split off to become Bangladesh). Given deep feelings of national insecurity, Pakistani politicians were not reluctant to play the religion card. Economic and cultural instability strengthened the forces of social conservatism. In place of "multiple truth claims," there emerged a seeking for "single visions." The foundations were laid for Pakistan today, a society in which violence and intolerance seem all but out of control.

This is not only – or even primarily – a religious matter, although Islam is a convenient weapon for the forces of reaction. Instead, as one of the people at the workshop argued, Pakistan is now pervaded at all levels by a "culture of gangsterism." If pluralism remains at all, it takes the form of a pluralistic diffusion of violence to every stratum of society and corner of the land.

What to do? The workshop participants included several activists, fresh from the trenches. (Fouzia Saeed's work with abused women through the Bedari center here in Islamabad is an example.) The consensus, though, was that treating symptoms is not enough; rather, the deeper causes of the problems have to be addressed. This implies a series of actions to loosen up state ideologies (especially the looming Islamicization of politics), to address the personal and social insecurities that lead people to simplify and harden their outlook, and to provide alternative interpretations of Islamic teachings. The educational system (curriculum, texts, teaching methods) and the media would be entry points for trying to bring about change.

This won't bring Samia back, and it won't save the next Samia. Still, there was something so sweet and so true in the discussion over these two days that one can only look with hope for what might come next, and seek ways to help.

*   *   *

There was a piece by Muzaffar Iqbal on the "Opinion" page of the latest *News*, "Death of a thinking man." The thinking man had been a friend of Iqbal's, a professor fallen prey to the cynical politics of his university and of Pakistan. Shortly before his death, the thinking man said to Iqbal: "Go around the country and try to find someone who can still think. You will have to look hard, but you will find one. Once you have found such a person, you will have found a miniature of hell."

*   *   *

I went to the ceremonial concluding session this evening of a Bedari training workshop on crisis intervention. After they passed out the certificates of participation, the woman who directed the film *Inteha*, Samina Pirzada, talked about her life and her work. What she had to say was simple enough: we have to learn to love each other, to break free from patterns of abuse. In Pakistan just now, that kind of message can get you in big trouble.

Inteha, which appeared earlier this year, borrows the conventions of Pakistani filmmaking: song, suggestive dance, men fighting, implied rape (viewed as wrong but titillating). The difference is that in *Inteha*, the rape is of a woman by her husband. Nothing like this had happened in Pakistani films before, and the laying bare of what is common domestic violence here created a furor when the film appeared. *Inteha* somehow slipped past the censors, but the Minister of Information then tried to ban it anyway. According to Kamran, the ensuing, very Pakistani forms of coercion and unpleasantness left Samina in an emotional state where she could hardly leave the house without being held upright.

When they showed some clips from the film, I found myself watching Samina watching what she had created. It was almost unbearable – clearly, it was as hard for her to see the rape scene for the nth time as it must have been to conceive and direct it in the first place. When I told her this afterward, she touched my arm in a gesture of gratefulness.

Our friend Kamran has brought me together with people (he is one, Samina another) whose lives have such gravity and such radiance. There is grace at work here.

*   *   *

In Angola, there were never any birds. Well, that's not strictly true: there was the egret-tree I passed on the way to work one morning in Luanda. That was magic, though; it never happened again, and it doesn't really count.

Islamabad is different. If you sit on our second-floor terrace on a sunny winter day, it is like being in an aviary. The whole world is birds and the sounds of birds as far as you can hear, the flash as they burst out of a nearby tree and skim away on a rushed errand, the complicated trajectory as they return, all lightning approach and midair right-angle turns and last-second deceleration for a soft landing on an obscured branch somewhere inside the canopy of leaves. Birds' reflexes are almost unimaginably quick, and they can do anything: take off straight up, hover. I haven't actually seen these flying backwards, but it wouldn't surprise me if they did.

We have the winter birds now. I scatter breadcrumbs across the terrace and settle back to watch. First out of the line of trees on the kitchen side of the house are the sparrows (described in our bird book as "cheeky town dwellers," which is close enough – one of them has taken to fluttering down to the kitchen window ledge when I appear for breakfast to remind me that they are hungry too). The sparrows are joined by several squawky, yellow-eyed mynas, the next most cheeky bird we have. Then appear a couple of red-vented bulbuls, dark-crested and with a brilliant flash of red under their tails. The bird book calls the bulbuls "pugnacious" and says they can be trained as fighting birds, but on the terrace they are skittish and ever ready to retreat to the trees, once there calling melodiously to each other to decide on a next move. More skittish still are the house crows, strikingly ugly to the judging eye, who hop about on the far edge of the terrace wishing me to disappear so they can share in the feast.

Occasionally something less familiar passes through. This morning it was a pair of treepies (a smaller version of the red-billed blue magpies that live at higher elevations in Pakistan), eighteen inches of bird two-thirds of which is an awkwardly floppy double tail. (They are supposed to live on smaller birds, among other things, and I can only hope they are not after our sparrows.) In intermediate seasons we have hoopoes strolling on the lawn, all long curved bill and Indian headdress crest, but they must have headed south by now.

Overhead, other birds sweep by, usually in pairs, although there are also the high-flying flocks of brilliant-green parakeets, especially in that day-ending, busy time for birds in the hour before sunset. Higher still, small groups of pariah kites ride updrafts on motionless wings, tails cocked this way and that as rudders to loop through the thin sky, eyes as keen as any spy satellite watching everything below.

My favorites, though, are the cheeky sparrows. A flock of uncountable dozens has taken to roosting in the line of trees by the terrace. In late afternoon they begin to drift back from wherever they have been, lining up on the terrace railings or making forays into the trees to see if their perches are ready for the night. Eventually, they reach some critical bird mass within the branches and burst into a cacophony of twittering as if recounting the tales of the day. Finally, they nod off. When we come with a flashlight in the night, we can spot through the branches little puffballs of sparrow, feathers fluffed up and heads buried under wings, dead to the world. At dawn they wake up, twitter wildly in joy at the miracle of the rising sun, shake out their feathers, and head off to do whatever they do.

In my next incarnation, can I be a bird?

Chapter 14
NEW ZEALAND
2004

At the end of my assignment in Pakistan, I negotiated an early-retirement package with the World Food Program and moved to Ireland to be close to Tana and Alex. Dublin has to be one of the most expensive cities in which to live, though, and my pension dollars steadily lost value against the Irish pound (and then the Euro) the entire time I was there. Staying on seemed beyond my financial reach, so I decided to pack everything up and get on a plane for New Zealand, exactly halfway around the world and as far south of the equator as Ireland is north. With some work, I might be able to reconstruct why this seemed to make sense at the time. In the event, I discovered a beautiful country and within it Tarchin Hearn, the Buddhist ex-monk whose teachings on matters of body and spirit I've done my best to absorb since.

I've stumbled into a ten-day meditation retreat with someone named Tarchin Hearn at a center on the Coromandel Peninsula. Tarchin is originally from the UK, but he grew up in Toronto and later moved to New Zealand. He's been studying and practicing Buddhism since he was 19 (he's now in his mid-50s) and was a Karma Kagyu monk for 12 years.

Tarchin has the classic Buddhist texts and practices down cold, but he has a take on it all that is non-dogmatic and very accessible. There's a clarity to his teaching that can seem weightless until you realize how far it has penetrated.

I like the way he characterizes meditation: deep awareness, deep investigation, deep acceptance. I like the emphasis he puts on what the body is experiencing as we meditatively take in the world. (For practice, we do lots of walking meditation and a kind of Tibetan yoga called kum nye.) And I like the seeming whimsy with which he can make serious points:

> Visualize the quarter-moon above you, on its side like the smile of a Cheshire Cat. Gently falling from it like snowflakes are millions of tiny smiles. They fall into you, filling you (concentrating on the parts of the body where they are most needed), leaking out into the ground, where they spread and rise into the bodies of others around (whose smiles, of course, are rising into you).

A lot of the Buddhism I've been involved with could be rather arid. There's nothing arid about Tarchin. I've finally found my teacher.

*   *   *

One of my absolutely favorite movies is *Whale Rider*, the story of a young Maori girl who would be the natural choice for the next chief of her village except that… she's a girl. (The tale of how she eventually triumphs is quite wonderful.) The movie was filmed in Whangara, on the far eastern lip of New Zealand's North Island. Movie tourists drove the Maori there crazy, walking through their yards and banging on doors wanting to be entertained and wandering around the communal meeting grounds with their shoes on – hardcore wrongness – so the villagers took down the "Whangara" sign on Route 35 as it winds its way from Gisborne up the coast toward the East Cape lighthouse, and you have to know to turn at the "Pa Road" sign instead.

From there you drive several miles through rolling country, past the school where parts of the movie take place, hugging the back of a steep hill and emerging at an overlook, the village spread out below. You're asked not to go past that point, so you pull off the road, get out, and start to look.

It's another perfect New Zealand half-moon bay, cradled in rugged hills half-meadow half-forest, empty beach curling around its perimeter. Just offshore to the north, far away and indistinct, are dark shapes in the water: rocks? whales? This is where the scenes with the whales on the beach were filmed, and rumor has it that the crew left some of their whales behind when they finished, so it's hard to be sure.

Below is the village, perhaps 20 nondescript houses separated by low fences and lots of grass, greener than I remember from the movie. There are no adults in sight, but children cross the lawns, move along the lanes, disappear again.

Then, on the southern edge of the settlement, I notice a pitched red roof through a gap in the trees. At the peak on the ocean end is a carving of a man straddling a whale – a memorable image from the movie. It's Paikea the Whale Rider, who according to tradition rode a whale to New Zealand from Hawaiki, the mythological original homeland of the Maori.

I'm flooded with feelings from the movie, from other things I've read since about Paikea, from seeing him now in this place where he's always been, long before Witi Ihimaera wrote the book *Whale Rider* about him, even longer before the movie was made. Here is the ancestor of everyone in Whangara, looking out to sea in hopes that the ancients will come again, bringing healing to the wounded tribe.

It's getting cold now and the shadows are climbing up the walls of the meeting house toward Paikea; but an intuition of what he feels like to the people below is growing in me, and I can't move. I keep looking at the carving on the roof with a deepening sense of gratefulness, for what I'm not quite certain. The sun finally drops below the hills behind me, the spell is broken, and I head back to Gisborne.

Earlier in the day, I had been in a school of Maori art, being shown around by a woman who is weaving powerful forms as part of her studies. Alluding to the mythic meaning of the patterns she weaves into her pieces, she communicated something I had felt in talking with a woman in Rotorua about the importance of the Maori-language pre-school in her village, with a Maori police detective in Taupo about his need to return to his ancestral land, or with other people I've come across along the way. There's something extraordinary about Maori consciousness that isn't grasped in reading about it – you have to ex-perience it heart-to-heart. I only have a glimmering of what that is, but it touches places deep inside. I'm a lucky man.

*   *   *

You find Fox Glacier down the west coast of New Zealand's South Island, not far from the seaside village that is home to Keri Hulme, who wrote *The Bone People* there. The glacier began as the frozen tears of the lovely Hinehukatere, mourning Tawe, her lover, who had fallen to his death as they climbed the mountains together. The river of ice took a gouge out of the valley below and then, 14,000 years ago, retreated back into the mountains. Little by little, the hillsides turned to forest and the gouge filled with water, becoming what is now Lake Matheson.

I stand on a jetty extending into the lake, looking across the water to the snow-topped range of mountains that cradle the glacier. Rising above the rest is Mount Cook, whose peak – at more than 12,000 feet – is the highest point in New Zealand. A few degrees to the left, the frozen rush of the glacier emerges from the range. The panorama is vast, implacable, almost too much to take in.

Around me is a more graspable world. The lake's dark waters per-fectly mirror the mountains and the cottony clouds brushing against them. In the woods, birds plonk and twitter and squawk. Ducks paddle by. A bee works its way systematically through the tall reeds that fringe the boundary of the lake.

I start back toward my car through the moist intimacy of the trees. The water-laden winds from the Tasman Sea rise sharply when they reach this mountainous coast, dropping several yards of rain each year. Around the lake, only a few miles from the foot of the glacier, is rainforest.

By the side of the track is an ancient tree with a yard-high gash framed in black from a long-ago lightning strike. Extending from the gash around the curve of the tree is bare yellow wood, and then dense scatters of fern and moss on pebbled bark.

The gash itself is perhaps four inches wide and eight deep. If the mountains command awe through mass and majesty, the world inside the gash commands awe through the miniature perfection of its detail. At chest height, the most delicate of webs has been woven across it by a tiny orange spider, which scuttles away from my shadow and disappears into a crack in the tree. The invisible remnants of old webs deeper inside have caught countless flecks of bark that rest suspended in mid-fall like a puzzle waiting to be solved. Among the flecks, a sliver trembles in the faintest of breezes like a fairy wind chime.

The back wall of the gash is made from grainy strips of inner tree, a complex texturing like a cavern deep in the earth. Golden stalactites have formed from the drip of sap in the wounded tree, and I half expect to spot pea-sized bats darting among them. In one corner is another web, denser and thicker than the first. It hollows in the middle to create a curving tube the width of a finger to lure curious insects irreversibly within. Behind the tube's wall I can see a round black belly, the maker waiting patiently for its meal.

I realize the spiders have registered my presence as I have theirs, and the same must have happened as I intersected with the bee and the ducks and the woods birds. The ferns and I breathed each other's air. When I earlier walked to the foot of the glacier, my body heat melted a drop of ice.

There is so infinitely much happening here. Creatures pause, shift trajectory, subtly reshape their day because they've noticed me – with what result? The fern grows imperceptibly faster and the glacier imperceptibly slower. My lingering in response to what I see means that I make it only to Ross instead of Hokitika by the end of the day – again, with what result?

We are accumulations of millions of forces and moments like these, and the effects are incalculable: the gash in a tree birthed a world that slowed me down so I stayed in a Ross B&B whose owner had to provide me breakfast the next morning and left later than planned for an appointment with the strands of our conversation in his head (with what result?), ripples of interbeing spreading through time and space because of (among a million things more) a long-ago lightning strike on a tree on a hill left by a glacier in retreat, all that the results of a million other moments of interbeing. We are so utterly contingent.

And so utterly responsible. We stand endlessly where countless shifting ripples have converged to make this moment, and the next, and the next, sending off new ripples to shape new moments for everything we touch. Nothing is so trivial we can afford to let it pass unnoticed – if the butterfly flapping its wings in Costa Rica can cause a typhoon in Vietnam, what might come of a diverted bee at Lake Matheson? What we do is mediated by so many other forces that its effects quickly pass beyond our control, and yet we need to act as mindfully as we can in hopes of doing no harm, perhaps even sending healing into the turbulent interbeing of things.

This is obvious enough, but dullness and inertia can take over, keeping us from noticing. Falling in love is a way to break through to fresh awareness and wonder, to a wanting to be skillful in word and touch. Traveling does this too, at least for a time. (Eventually, as I know, change of scene becomes routine, and the dullness creeps in again. That can happen with love, too.) Ultimately, the light of awareness has to be found within, not startled into being by a glimpse of wonder outside. Still, I am deeply grateful to the glacier and the lake and the birds and the life inside the gash in the tree (and to love) for reminding me of what I am capable of knowing.

* * *

More interbeing. I'm at Cape Reinga, on the tip of the North Island:

Behind me, the lighthouse at the top of New Zealand.
To the left, the Tasman Sea.
To the right, the Pacific Ocean.
Where these two great waters meet
are complex flows of gravely rolling waves
moving to each other from odd angles.

The waves touch, swelling, and enter each other,
countless drops tremoring together,
knowing Ocean,
while the waves keep moving, pass beyond each other,
subtly different,
wiser than before.

Suddenly, as I'm taking this in, *I remember how it feels.* It can happen in a moment of intense connection with another person, aware of being wave and knowing Ocean. It is most commonly love that gets us there. Meditation helps.

*   *   *

There's a Maori concept called "mana" that I'm trying to get my mind around. The dictionaries define "mana" in terms such as power, vitality, authority, or psychic force; but I'm warned (most recently by a woman who teaches a course on Maori mana at a university here) that you can't snatch at English words, you have to be grounded in the culture within which mana arises. I'm therefore approaching this softly softly, asking everyone I talk with (Maori when possible) what the word means.

My suspicion (hope?) is that there is a relationship between mana and some of the glimpses into suchness that I've gotten in my Buddhist work. Thich Nhat Hanh talks about suchness (or tathata) as a term meaning "true nature": "Everything has a suchness; that is how we recognize it. An orange has its suchness; that is why we don't confuse it with a lemon." My deepest understanding of the suchness of things came in the convulsions of a long retreat I did in southern France in 2001, when I ended up engaged with the suchness of a tree as a reaction against the Madhyamikan anti-"tree" dogmas we were being fed. Was it the tree's mana I was experiencing?

(An earlier gut experience of what suchness entails came years back when I saw Richard Burton conjugate the verb "to be" on a TV documentary – you take your glimpses into the deepest reality where you find them...)

Objects and places can apparently have mana as well. I thought of this the other day when I was at a lookout at the edge of Lake Papaitonga, south of Levin on the North Island's west coast. I was watching the black swans and their cygnets being serene when I suddenly realized there was great energy radiating from a wooded hill to one side. I don't know how other people experience these energies, but I feel them as a physical action on my torso, between heart and belly. (It's the feeling I had with a hill I came across in Scotland last year.) When I later read through the information at the entrance to the reserve, it turned out this was a sacred area, so there may have been "tapu" (which has to do with the specifically sacred) rather than "mana" at work. These forces must be related somehow, but I'm far from knowing how.

It's so nice to be on the edges of deep material I don't understand. One of the things that was killing me about being a food aid bureaucrat toward the end was that I understood most of what was going on about as well as I could (and much better than the system could tolerate). There were new areas I might profitably have explored – the Tao of the bureaucracy in terms of its interpersonal flows, for example – but I got stuck and couldn't do it. I'm unsticking a bit now, and none too soon. At best, you end up a wise and compassionate being. At worst, you have a lot of fun.

*   *   *

I think I've been living a dream. My four months in New Zealand were rich beyond anything I could have imagined. I found a teacher who cuts to the deepest heart of how I feel and understand things, with whom I've already spent time clearing brush and shaping paths through his woods as well as taking in his teachings, and who is leading a six-month retreat I'll gratefully enter next year. I've made friends (or deepened friendships) that will be mine for life, and that have changed my life. I've experienced such beauty – seals playing in perfect bays, glaciers emerging from snow-capped mountains, trees heavy with nesting cormorants (or, as they're delightfully known here, pied shags), pairs of saucy fantails, rolling emerald meadows grazed by cows or sheep or deer, the many worlds in the mottled bark of a Tanekaha tree in the forests of Coromandel.

Some of these moments have far transcended mere beauty: the realization, watching the Pacific meet the Tasman Sea, of how we flow through each other; the deep experience of interbeing that came from standing with a lightning-struck tree near Fox Glacier; the sense of energy radiating from a sacred hill south of Levin. I'd been overwhelmed by the simple power of *Whale Rider* before I left Dublin, but had no idea in how many ways I'd intersect with Maoritanga along the way: the Maori detective in Taupo describing his need to return to his birthplace and his people (to hear a Maori talk about "our people" is to have a brief window into a wholly different way of experiencing the world), the professor I'm still exchanging emails with about core Maori views of things, the discoveries in the Maori collections of the Tauranga library and the Wanganui Museum, the slightly edgy jazz within a long meeting with a Maori carver who wanted to talk about Buddhism and biofeedback, my pilgrimages to the places where *Whale Rider* was filmed and *The Bone People* was written.

I've also brushed the edges of lives all over New Zealand, notably in dozens of hours of warm talk with the people running the B&Bs where I've stayed: the former commander in the New Zealand navy (now in Waipu growing orchids for export to Canada and Japan) and the former fighter pilot in Masterton (when I was four years old in Washington, D.C., he was based there testing American planes for the British air force); the Israeli woman in Wellington whose 15-year-old adopted daughter recently ran away from home for six weeks and was finally arrested when she split from a babysitting job and took the baby with her; the woman in Pukenui whose first husband had died of brain cancer and whose 26-year-old daughter had a stroke in Bangkok after a flight from the U.K. (she's now 28 with a new baby) – her husband and I swapped Big Sur stories, his involving a head-on collision with a bus that left him for weeks in a Monterey hospital (perhaps unsurprisingly, there was something askew about the vibes in their place); the gentle couple in Omapere (former farmer, former teacher) who hadn't traveled much but were about to take off for a three-week Silk Route tour through China and Uzbekistan (or so they thought – they weren't quite sure); the woman who manages Telstra's computers in Levin and whose husband had been a psychiatric nurse for 27 years (he had a watchful, restless energy that could have come with the territory). The varieties of human experience are so limitless; the courage of beings in moving through their experience is so profound.

I may be leaving at just the right moment – I feel so opened by the process (exposed, awake) and so blessed by what I've passed though in that state (all this in four months?); perhaps it's time to let that settle into my cells and go on to whatever the U.S. and Ireland bring. Then back...

EPILOGUE

In 2005, I returned to New Zealand for a six-month retreat with my newfound teacher Tarchin and his companion, Mary, in the hills of the South Island. It was the longest of dozens of mostly Buddhist retreats I've been part of since 1999 in the U.S., Ireland, Canada, England, France, and New Zealand. What Buddhism (and before that Catholicism) has meant to me is the subject of another book. Here, perhaps I only need say that Buddhism has involved as many journeyings inward as my other travels took me outward.

In 2006, I returned to the U.S. after a quarter-century living elsewhere. Most of my travels in the years since have been within the U.S. (East, West, Midwest, South) or off to Ireland (spending time with children and grandchildren), Italy (for Alex's wedding), the U.K. (visiting friends), and Barcelona (to take in the Gaudis), along with periods of retreat in Canada and New Zealand.

More than a half-century of travel has meant various things for me. First, it was a way of shaking me loose from lazy patterns of living that otherwise kept me half-asleep. When I moved from Rome to Eritrea in 1995, for example, I wrote of my work, "There are things here I cannot do from memory, and I love the zest of that." Settling in a new place (in a new country, perhaps in a new job), you need to discover much of life anew (how and where to shop, do laundry, eat out, maneuver through a day in the office, vacation; with whom to do these things). You have to look around and pay attention. People of higher spiritual accomplishment can do this in the fresh moment of each new day in the same place; I needed a greater jolt from time to time.

Being ever in new contexts also gave me perspective on the old ones. Somewhere along the way, I wrote:

There are no roads out of this place.
I have tried them all, and each time
I return to where I started.
Still, each road is its own place.
Each has its own view, and each time
I see more clearly the place where I arrive.

It was my own version of T. S. Eliot writing in *Four Quartets*:

We shall not cease from exploration
And the end of all our exploring
Will be to arrive where we started
And know the place for the first time.

You know the place so well because you see it from outside, a privileged vantage point for gaining clarity. It can get you in trouble. In her book *Lost in Translation* (no relation to the 2003 movie), Eva Hoffman describes what she found in Canada and the U.S. as a young immigrant from Eastern Europe. She became a critic of what she saw around her. Writing about her time at Harvard, she says, "In the counternorms my peers profess, I perceive the structure of the norms they ostensibly reject, inverted like an underwater reflection, but still recognizable. Much of the time, I'm in a rage. Immigrant rage, I call it... I think my friends often suspect me of a perverse refusal to play along, an unaccountable desire to provoke and disturb their comfortable consensus."

Being so much away from the U.S. made me something of an immigrant each time I returned, and I know what immigrant rage feels like. When I wrote my article about the communes movement for *The New York Times Magazine* in 1971, for example, my main (somewhat angry) observation was that the core values of the then "counterculture" were much the same as those of the culture people claimed to be countering. Not everybody wants that kind of thing pointed out to them.

EPILOGUE

Being everywhere something of an outsider affected my work life as well. Any large workplace will create its own culture, largely devoted to preserving and extending itself. In international development and humanitarian aid organizations, to thrive requires giving the appearance of doing a good job so that donors will keep providing resources. The organizations don't actually have to *do* useful things for their ostensible beneficiaries, since they evaluate their own work and come to conclusions that will appeal to the donors. Lacking any independent reality check, it becomes comforting for the people within such workplaces to believe the image they have created of their work.

A newcomer not yet caught up in the prevailing culture is likely to see disparities between the organization's myths and the realities on the ground. The travel notes above document a lot of that kind of tension: a major, wholly hallucinatory U.N. drought-relief-cum-development activity in the Sudan; Potemkin community development activities in India; the U.N.'s fantasy of "demobilizing" rebel soldiers in Angola; the chasm between the way the "experts" viewed watershed management in Nepal and the way farmers lived their lives; the radical disconnect between the real world and the imaginings of a Chief Forestry Officer in Malawi. My outsider observations on flights of fancy like these were often seen by my colleagues as an unaccountable desire to provoke and disturb their comfortable consensus.

It's not the frustrations of being an outsider that remain most vivid from all those years, though. There are so many people to remember. I wrote from Eritrea about the kinds of expatriates you meet along the way, "the saints and whiskey priests and expatriate project managers, the free-lance 'journalists' and burnouts, the radically displaced." We expatriates were pretty much all radically displaced, including people like Anne and Barbara and David and Becky and Arnulf in Eritrea, Chris and Lennart and Sakaria in the Sudan, Jane and Mons in Ethiopia, Signore Gregori in Nepal, the Dutchman on the Nile river boat, Nick and Paul and Howard and the boys from the Halo Trust in Angola, Bronek in Pakistan.

Equally memorable were the people who called those places home: Mrs. Hoa and Madame Minh in Vietnam, Anna and Dr. Nerayo and Dawit in Eritrea, Yeraswork in Ethiopia, the Sudanese with the Christian service organization in Khartoum, Earnest and Mrs. Mabaso and Mr. Mkoola and so many more in Malawi, Senhora Palmira and my grouchy neighbors and Serafim and the boy with the bullet in his stomach in Angola, Kamran and Gulzar and Fouzia and Samina in Pakistan, the Maori (a detective, a professor, a carver) in New Zealand.

Then there are people like Tarchin and Mary and the B&B owners in New Zealand, a category of their own, not quite natives, not quite outsiders.

I try to encompass all of them in one vast spaciousness of recollection. It's as if we had been partners in a great dance extending over decades through every continent, moving together in various combinations, touching, dancing away again. In my field of memory, each partner in turn takes center stage, seamlessly of the dance but unfathomably complex and individual. Such beauty, such perfection.

Travels with David.

CPSIA information can be obtained at www.ICGtesting.com
Printed in the USA
BVOW01s1933050816

458123BV00002B/13/P